ANSWERING ★ THE CRY FOR FREEDOM

STORIES OF AFRICAN AMERICANS AND THE AMERICAN REVOLUTION

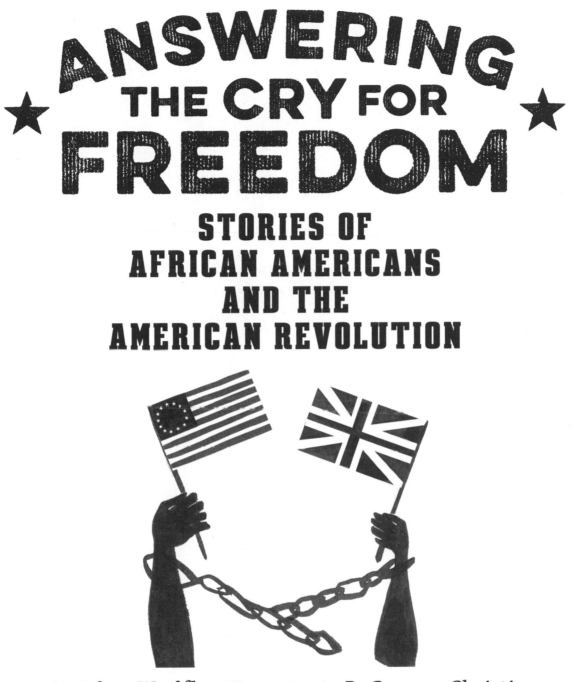

Gretchen Woelfle   *Illustrations by* R. Gregory Christie

CALKINS CREEK

AN IMPRINT OF ASTRA BOOKS FOR YOUNG READERS

NEW YORK

Calkins Creek
An imprint of Astra Books for Young Readers,
a division of Astra Publishing House
astrapublishinghouse.com
Printed in China

ISBN: 978-1-62979-306-1 (hardcover)
ISBN: 978-1-62979-744-1 (eBook)

Library of Congress Control Number: 2016932168

First edition

10 9 8 7 6

Design by William Mack
Titles set in Eveleth and Archive Kludsky
Text set in Dederon Serif
The illustrations are done in ink on paper.

To Alice, Cleo, and Oskar
and to all young people working for social and
environmental justice. You give me inspiration in the
present and hope for the future.
—GW

For Jimmy Summers, my brother in spirit.
—RGC

CONTENTS

INTRODUCTION

A HIDDEN CHAPTER OF THE AMERICAN REVOLUTION

In 1775, when the American Revolution began and colonists took up arms to free themselves from British rule, slavery existed in every one of the thirteen colonies. In 1776, when the Founding Fathers signed the Declaration of Independence, declaring that "all men" were entitled to "life, liberty, and the pursuit of happiness," they didn't really mean everyone. The American Patriots did not fight to give life, liberty, and basic civil rights to five hundred thousand African Americans enslaved in the North and South. Yet African Americans living in Boston, where Patriot passions blazed, and those living on isolated southern plantations heard talk about liberty and equality.

And those ideas were as contagious as smallpox.

In 1775 and again in 1779, the British issued a proclamation offering freedom to slaves owned by Patriots. Hundreds, then thousands of men, women, and children fled to British army territory—

and freedom. Sixty thousand African Americans became Black Loyalists—loyal to Great Britain—because this was their best chance for freedom.

George Washington understood their choice. He wrote: "Liberty, when it begins to take root, is a plant of rapid growth." Among African Americans, the "liberty plant" took root in many places, in many ways. Most slaves in the American colonies did not flee to the British during the Revolution. But they sought freedom in other ways: by joining the Continental army, by buying their freedom from their owners, and by running away. Then came their struggle for equality.

This book tells the story of a hidden chapter of the American Revolution: how African Americans answered the Revolution's cry for freedom. The thirteen people in this book include men and women, free and enslaved, northern and southern, African-born and American-born; soldiers, preachers, farmers, merchants, housekeepers, a sea captain, and a poet. It describes the risks they took, the hardships they faced, and the victories they won.

Four of these people wrote their autobiographies. A few more wrote letters, speeches, and poems. Others were described in interviews and essays. One left only his name and scraps of information on official lists and documents.

To learn more about these people, I traveled from Virginia to Nova Scotia to visit plantations, towns, and cities to find their traces. Some became influential leaders. Some ventured far from home. Many worked to end racial oppression. Others lived quiet lives, known only to friends and family.

But these African Americans of the Revolutionary era—the ones who remained in America and the ones who sailed away with the British after the war—shared a vision. They had heard the claim that all people are free and equal . . . and they believed it.

★ PART ONE ★

FIGHTING A WAR FOR FREEDOM

When the American colonies went to war against Great Britain in April 1775, young men—and many not so young—flocked to join the fight. Each colony had its own troops, called militias, but the American Revolution saw something new: a Continental army drawn from all thirteen colonies. In the north, freemen, black and white, enlisted.

But not for long.

In July 1775, General George Washington, commander in chief of the Continentals and a Virginia slave owner, bowed to pressure from his fellow southerners in the Continental Congress and barred any more African Americans from joining the army.

By December 1775, realizing that he needed all the men he could get, Washington persuaded Congress to let free African Americans enlist. No enslaved soldiers, though. Slave owners feared that armed slaves, desperate for freedom, would turn their guns on their masters.

BLACK LOYALISTS

While the American Patriots squabbled about blacks in their army, Lord Dunmore, British royal governor of Virginia, promised freedom to slaves who escaped from their Patriot masters and joined the British. Hundreds of men, women, and children fled to his camp. He took them all in, those who could serve in the army and those who couldn't, and they became Black Loyalists.

BLACK PATRIOT SOLDIERS

As the war dragged on year after year, the state militias could not fill their quotas of soldiers. Beginning in 1777, northern states began to adopt new policies. White men could send their slaves to fight in their place. Some owners promised these substitute soldiers freedom after the war. Some states passed laws that allowed enslaved men to enlist, promising them freedom if they survived. But only able-bodied young men were given this chance; enslaved women, children, and old men were out of luck. At one point, the Continental Congress, in need of soldiers, asked South Carolina and Georgia to recruit three thousand slaves for the Continental army. The two states wouldn't even consider it, fearing violence from armed slaves.

In 1778–80, the British army captured Savannah, Georgia, and Charleston and Camden, South Carolina. British general Sir Henry Clinton repeated Lord Dunmore's promise: "All Negroes that fly from the enemy's country are free. No person whatever can claim a right to them. Whoever sells them shall be prosecuted with the utmost severity." Thousands more fled to freedom by joining the British army.

BLACK AND WHITE FIGHTING TOGETHER

For the first few years of the war, both the British and Continental armies used African Americans not as fighting men but as officers' servants or as "pioneers," who dug fortifications, foraged for food and supplies, and repaired roads and bridges. African American women served the British army, too, as cooks, laundresses, and servants. By the end of the war, though, African American men fought alongside white men on both sides. They suffered and died in battle and in the dreadful epidemics that plagued both armies. A seven-year smallpox epidemic stalked the armies wherever they marched and killed more people than enemy bullets.

Despite the many terrible hardships, African American men chose to go to war for freedom—their own and their countrymen's.

THREE SOLDIERS

Boston King, an enslaved South Carolinian, escaped to the British army, gained his freedom, and fought for his liberators. After the war, he moved first to Canada, then to Africa, using his freedom to reinvent himself several times in his "pursuit of happiness."

Agrippa Hull, born free, joined the Continental army in 1777 when he was eighteen and served until the war ended, six years later. He traveled thousands of miles away from home, served under famous Revolutionary heroes, and witnessed large-scale slavery in the south. When he returned home to Stockbridge, Massachusetts, after the war, he recounted his war stories for the rest of his long life. Massachusetts had abolished slavery in 1783, but Hull helped slaves escaping from nearby New York State.

James Armistead Lafayette, enslaved in Virginia, joined the Continental army and became a spy for the Americans, then a double agent. When the war ended, James remained enslaved but continued his fight for his liberty with the help of the Marquis de Lafayette.

The Revolution's cry for freedom inspired them all.

CHAPTER ONE

BOSTON KING

(ca. 1760–1802)

Boston King sat at his desk at Kingswood School in Bristol, England, and stared at a stack of blank paper. Friends had urged him to write the story of his life, but how to begin? He was used to preaching sermons, but writing a book was another matter. King was lucky to know how to read and write, for few American slaves learned those skills.

Boston King had been many things in his thirty-four years: carpenter, British soldier, Nova Scotia fisherman, Methodist preacher, emigrant from the United States to Canada and later to Africa. His life had been one dangerous adventure after another, and his spiritual life had been full of turmoil. Boston's father led family prayers during his son's childhood, but it was many years before Boston called himself a good Christian. Should he write about his spiritual struggles or his worldly adventures?

He would tell it all.

He picked up a quill pen and began to write: *Memoirs of the Life of Boston King, a Black Preacher. Written by Himself, during his Residence at Kingswood School.*

As a boy, Boston had privileges other enslaved children didn't. His parents held important jobs on Richard Waring's rice plantation near Charleston, South Carolina. Boston's father had charge of the slaves who worked in the fields. His mother worked as a seamstress and nursed the other slaves. Boston had woods to explore, a river to swim in, and hills to roll down until he got dizzy.

"MY FATHER WAS STOLEN AWAY FROM AFRICA WHEN HE WAS YOUNG."

—*Boston King*

Boston's mother may have used scraps of fine cotton left over from the Waring family's clothes to make his shirts and trousers. Other enslaved children wore rough linen or woolen clothes. Boston would have spent his days with his mother in the big house. Other children stayed in the slave quarters while their parents worked in the rice fields. When Boston was six, he began running errands for his master. From the big house to the storage sheds to the stables, Boston would roam, carrying messages and bundles.

At age nine, he began tending cattle with older boys. From them he learned "the horrible sin of Swearing and Cursing." It was all good fun until one night he "dreamt that the world was on fire," and God sent sinners tumbling from the gates of heaven "into the greatest despair and confusion." That scared Boston so much that he quit swearing and "bad company."

CARPENTER'S APPRENTICE

When Boston was sixteen, his owner, Richard Waring, apprenticed him to a carpenter in nearby Charleston. Learning a skilled trade

"I DREAMT THAT THE WORLD WAS ON FIRE, AND THAT I SAW THE SUPREME JUDGE DESCEND ON HIS GREAT WHITE THRONE!"

—*Boston King*

would make the young man more valuable to Waring. It would also give Boston opportunities to make his own money by working evenings and Sundays. He might even buy his freedom someday.

But the carpenter was a brutal man who "beat me severely, striking me upon the head, or any other part without mercy," Boston wrote. When other apprentices wrongly accused him of stealing, he was beaten so badly he couldn't work for weeks. Waring threatened to take him back to the plantation and the carpenter never whipped him again. "I began to acquire a proper knowledge of my trade," King wrote.

He was on his way to becoming a master carpenter, and these skills would serve him well in years to come.

CHOOSING FREEDOM

In May 1780, the British army captured Charleston, and Boston faced a hard choice. The British offered freedom to slaves, and now was his chance! But if he fled, he'd never see his family again. If Britain lost the war, the British might abandon him to slavery. It was a gamble: slavery in the world that he knew or freedom in a dangerous, unknown world.

Twenty-year-old Boston chose freedom. "I determined to . . . throw myself into the hands of the English. They received me readily, and I began to feel the happiness of liberty, of which I knew nothing before."

"I BEGAN TO FEEL THE HAPPINESS OF LIBERTY, OF WHICH I KNEW NOTHING BEFORE."

The privileges he had known as a child and the protection he received from Waring were nothing compared to freedom. Now he could choose his own path in life.

He was also free to choose a new name. Slave owners' account books listed first names only. Freed slaves chose a family name thoughtfully. Some took their masters' names as a link to their past. Boston chose to honor the British ruler and named himself Boston King. He joined the British army as a free Black Loyalist.

LIFE IN THE BRITISH ARMY

King's newfound "happiness of liberty" vanished a few weeks later when he caught smallpox. This deadly disease raged through the country from 1775 to 1782, spread by soldiers on the march. Smallpox killed more than 130,000 people, more than all the battles of the war. Luckily for King, an English soldier, his first white friend, nursed him back to health and helped save his life. Later, when the Englishman was wounded, King cared for him in the hospital, "rejoicing that it was in my power to return him the kindness he had shewed [me]."

King tramped through the mountains and swamps of North and South Carolina with the army. Once, when his company was surrounded, he crept thirty miles through enemy lines to a British outpost to get help. He survived ambushes, sieges, bloody battles, capture by the enemy, and escape back to Charleston.

LIVING FREE IN NEW YORK

When British forces withdrew from Charleston in 1782, King took passage on a British ship to New York City, the British army headquarters. He joined thousands more freed slaves there and met Violet, a refugee from North Carolina. Enslaved couples were forbidden to marry legally in the south. But now, in New York under British rule, Violet and Boston King were married.

Life in New York seemed safer, but not easier. King tried to find work as a carpenter, but he owned no tools. He became a house servant, "but the wages were so low that I was not able to keep myself in clothes," he wrote. He found another place as a servant but was cheated out of his wages.

Ever resourceful, he took a job on a pilot boat, guiding ships into the harbor. All was well until he was captured by the crew of an American ship. King's freedom meant nothing to them; he was a Loyalist—an enemy to America—and a runaway slave. They sold Boston King to a man in New Jersey.

ENSLAVED AGAIN

King never revealed the name of his new owner, only that he gave King meat once a day and milk twice a day. Even better, in the evenings he could attend school to learn to read the Bible. "But alas," wrote King, "all these enjoyments could not satisfy me without liberty!"

Freedom lay just across the Raritan River in New York, but so did danger. One slave caught trying to escape was jailed with arms and legs locked in the stocks day and night. King wrote, "This was a terrifying sight to me, as I expected to meet with the same kind of treatment, if taken in the act of attempting to regain my liberty."

What to do? He could remain enslaved in fairly comfortable conditions or make a run for freedom. Once again, he chose freedom.

In the middle of the night, he slipped past two guards on the shore and waded into the water. He heard one guard say, "I am sure I saw a man cross the river."

King froze until he heard the other reply, "There is no such thing."

"WE SAW OUR OLD MASTERS COMING . . . AND SEIZING UPON THEIR SLAVES IN THE STREETS OF NEW-YORK."

During the night, King crept through the marshes along the shore, waited for low tide, then waded across the river to Staten Island. He couldn't walk across New York Harbor, though. The sun would soon be up and he would be caught by watchmen on American ships anchored in the harbor. He crept along the shore and finally managed to steal a small boat, elude the watchmen, and row back to New York City. "My friends rejoiced to see me once more restored to liberty," he wrote.

That liberty was threatened again after the British surrendered to the Americans in 1783. Talk ran through New York that the freed slaves would be sent back to their former owners. King wrote: "This dreadful rumour filled us all with inexpressible anguish and terror, especially when we saw our old masters coming . . . and seizing upon their slaves in the streets of New-York." Boston and Violet hid from the slave catchers and put their trust in the British. They were rewarded when the British refused to return the Black Loyalists to slavery.

STARTING OVER IN NOVA SCOTIA

King, his wife, and three thousand other Black Loyalists sailed to Nova Scotia, a British colony on the east coast of Canada, in the summer of 1783. The couple received Certificates of Freedom along with a spade, an ax, 2 yd woolen cloth, 7 yd linen, 2 pairs stockings, 1 pair mitts, and one pair of shoes. Not much to build a new life in the wilderness.

The British promised them farmland and provisions for a year, and King, twenty-three years old, set to work building a home before the harsh Canadian winter set in. He found that his "farmland" was dense forest—the soil thin, growing seasons short, and harvests poor. So he and Violet, along with many other Black Loyalists, went to work for a time as servants for some of the twenty-seven thousand White Loyalists who had fled the United States. Few other jobs were available.

Though the Black Loyalists were poor in worldly goods, they had a rich religious life. Boston and Violet King had met Methodist minister Moses Wilkinson in New York. Daddy Moses, as he was called, blinded and crippled by smallpox, became the most popular preacher in Nova Scotia. His rousing sermons encouraged joyful shouting, singing, and foot stomping.

Violet King became a fervent Methodist, but Boston was tormented by doubts about his own sinful nature. Back and forth he swung between fear and faith. Several times he thought he heard a voice, perhaps God, whisper in his ear, "Peace be unto you," and that voice finally won him over. "All my doubts and fears vanished away: I saw, by faith, heaven opened to my view; and Christ and his holy angels rejoicing over me."

"I SAW, BY FAITH, HEAVEN OPENED TO MY VIEW; AND CHRIST AND HIS HOLY ANGELS REJOICING OVER ME."

King's Methodist friends urged him to preach to them, but he "was conscious of my great ignorance and insufficiency for a work of such importance." They insisted and he finally gave in. Daily prayer meetings in the settlers' homes gave him plenty of chances to preach and pray and tell the story of his doubts, fears, voices, and salvation.

HARD TIMES

Preaching was not a paying job, and King scraped together a living however he could. One harsh winter, food supplies nearly ran out and some people even starved to death. Boston King, whose strength and determination had helped him survive in wartime and escape from slavery, walked from town to town looking for work. At last, a man hired him to build a wooden chest, and King worked all night and delivered the chest

"BEING PINCHED WITH HUNGER AND COLD, I FELL DOWN SEVERAL TIMES, THRO' WEAKNESS, AND EXPECTED TO DIE ON THE SPOT."

the next morning. The man didn't like it, refused to pay, and ordered a different chest.

As King trudged the miles home through three feet of snow, "being pinched with hunger and cold, I fell down several times, thro' weakness, and expected to die on the spot." When he finally reached home, he found just one pint of cornmeal left for him and Violet. But the next day, he built the second chest, delivered it, and was paid in food. He sold the first chest to another man so his family could survive for a while longer.

News of King's carpentry skills spread, and luck began to favor him. Three fishermen hired King to build boats for them, and he earned enough to survive the winter. The following year, he built more boats and went on a fishing voyage for several months. He returned with barrels of mackerel and herring and money in his pocket—enough to buy Violet some new clothes.

Twenty-seven thousand White Loyalists had emigrated to Nova Scotia after the war. Not all of them fared as well as Boston King. As he saw it, their "distressing" financial state was

> owing to their great imprudence in building large houses, and striving to excel one another in this piece of vanity. When their money was almost expended, they began to build small fishing vessels; but alas, it was too late to repair their error . . . and [they] were compelled to flee to other parts of the continent.

Boston King was motivated not by vanity but by good sense and hard work. He preached to Methodists, both black and white, which brought him "great satisfaction." He again worked as a servant for "a gentleman, who gave me two shillings per day, with victuals [meals] and lodging; so that I was enabled to clothe myself and family, and provide other necessaries of life." King's carpentry skills brought some extra money for a few luxuries.

THE SIERRA LEONE COMPANY

In 1791, eight years after he had arrived in Nova Scotia, King heard a visiting white Englishman, John Clarkson, announce a plan to start a colony of former slaves in Sierra Leone, on the west coast of Africa. A group of abolitionists in London, England, had bought land there and formed the Sierra Leone Company. Africa had many natural resources that other countries needed, and they hoped that Black Loyalists could prosper as farmers and traders.

The settlers could also show Africans an honorable alternative to slave trading. Africans were both perpetrators and victims of the slave trade. They made war on neighboring tribes, captured their victims, and sold them to ships' captains who carried them to the Americas.

John Clarkson reported that Black Loyalists were the right sort of people for the Sierra Leone colony. "The majority of the men are better than any people in the labouring line of life in England: I would match them for strong sense, quick apprehension, clear reasoning, gratitude, affection for their wives & children, and friendship and good-will toward their neighbours." He seemed to be describing Boston King.

The abolitionists in London hoped that the Black Loyalists would help convert Africans to Christianity, and this inspired King. He had conquered many challenges in his life. Now he wanted to preach to and teach the Africans.

> *It was not for the sake of the advantages I hope to reap*
> *in Africa, which induced me to undertake the voyage,*
> *but from a desire that had long possessed my mind, of*
> *contributing to the best of my poor ability, in spreading*
> *the knowledge of Christianity in that country.*

ON TO AFRICA

Boston and Violet King sailed for Africa in January 1792, in one of the fifteen ships carrying twelve hundred settlers. For sixteen days, they endured violent storms. Many grew ill, and sixty-five passengers died. Violet King lay near death but survived to reach Sierra Leone.

In the new settlement called Freetown, the rainy season soon brought drenching downpours, thunder, lightning, and gale winds that blew off the thatched roofs of the houses the settlers had just built. They lived in a sea of mud that brought disease, and Violet King, still weak from the sea voyage, became sick with malaria and died. King hardly had time to grieve before he fell ill, but thanks to a strong body that had survived smallpox and famine, he fought off malaria.

Freetown was governed by a group of white Englishmen from London, and King worked for the English governor as a carpenter during the week. On Sundays, he preached to the Africans through an interpreter, but that wasn't enough for him. He wanted to teach and preach all week long.

When the governor appointed him as a teacher in a nearby African school, King had high hopes but limited success. He soon had twenty children in his school. He taught them English. He taught them to read. And he taught them the Lord's Prayer. But he couldn't convince the children's parents to come to church.

OFF TO ENGLAND

King worried that his lack of education was causing him to fail to convert the Africans. King could read, write, and preach, but he had had no formal schooling. When the governor, impressed with his dedication, offered to send him to school in England, King sailed away on the next ship.

If he believed he had shortcomings while in Africa, that belief grew stronger when he arrived in London and met "wise and judicious people, who were greatly my superiors in knowledge and understanding." He vowed never to show his "ignorance and inability," and when the English Methodists asked him to lead a service, he refused. After more urging, he finally climbed into the pulpit and spoke. Their praise touched his heart and he later wrote:

> *I found a more cordial love to the White People that I had ever experienced before. In the former part of my life I had suffered greatly from the cruelty and injustice of the Whites, which induced me to look upon them, in general as our enemies. . . . But on that day the Lord removed all my prejudices.*

He traveled on to Kingswood School in Bristol, a boarding school for sons of ministers, where "[I] endeavoured to acquire the knowledge I possibly could." Taking time out from his studies, he wrote his memoirs. He may have felt out of place, a man in his thirties, sharing a classroom with teenage boys, but he expressed only gratitude to the English Methodists: "I did not believe there were upon the face of the earth a people so friendly and human as I have proved them to be."

THE FINAL CHAPTER

After two years in England, King returned to Sierra Leone to his second wife Phillis and their three children. He found Freetown torn apart with political conflict, as the Nova Scotians fought with the English officials about how their town should be run. But King avoided the political wrangling and set off with his family on his final adventure: teaching and preaching to native Africans in outlying villages.

All his life, Boston King ventured forth, determined to shape his own destiny. He escaped from slavery, not once, but twice. Freedom brought its own challenges of poverty and survival in the harsh environments of Nova Scotia and Sierra Leone. But King managed to prosper. In his later years, he turned to the life of the mind and spirit, to teach the knowledge and understanding he had gained when he answered the cry for freedom.

CHAPTER TWO

AGRIPPA HULL

(1759–1848)

On the first of May 1777, Agrippa Hull walked from his family's farm to the nearby village of Stockbridge, Massachusetts. Purple trillium, yellow trout lilies, and white Dutchman's-breeches bloomed in the fields; springtime brought the promise of new life. Grippy, as his friends called him, had just turned eighteen and he was looking for a new life, too.

The American Revolution had been raging for two years, and Hull was eager to join the fight. A recruiting officer was set up at Isaac Marsh's tavern on Plain Street. Hull drew near to the tavern, ran up the steps, and into the hall. The officer asked a few questions, looked him over, and filled out some papers.

Agrippa Hull, 18 years old
Stature, 5 ft., 7 in.
complexion, black
hair, wool
Length of enlistment, a term of three years
or during the war [whichever was longer]
Payment for joining up: £15 10s.

Fifteen pounds, ten shillings! He had never seen so much money. Private Agrippa Hull of the First Stockbridge Company of Berkshire County, Massachusetts, was ready for the biggest adventure of his life.

Agrippa Hull always claimed that, before his father was sold into slavery and sent to America, he had been an African prince. There is no written record of this, but Amos and Bathsheba Hull had gained their freedom by the time their son, Agrippa, was born in Northampton, Massachusetts, on March 7, 1759. Freedom did not guarantee an easy childhood, though. Grippy's father died when he was two, and a few years later his mother couldn't manage their small plot of land alone. She had to sell it and walk from town to town with her young son, one of the many "strolling poor," looking for work wherever she could find it.

When Grippy was seven, his mother sent him to live with Joab and Rose Binney in Stockbridge, Massachusetts. This free black couple owned a fifty-acre farm and gave the boy a stable home and a chance to go to school to learn reading, writing, and arithmetic. Five years later, his mother and her new husband settled near Stockbridge, and Grippy returned to live on their small farm.

REVOLUTION!

In April 1775, across the colony, near Boston—a five-day journey on horseback—the Battle of Lexington and Concord pitted American militiamen against the British army. The American Revolution had begun. Grippy Hull was too young to enlist, so he bided his time on the farm. Two years later, when he turned eighteen, he and eleven other African Americans from Stockbridge joined the Continental army.

A soldier's life excited the young man. It gave him a chance to see the country and prove his bravery. Hull didn't get along with his stepfather, and soldiering was a good excuse to leave home. Money was an issue, too. His enlistment bonus was an enormous sum for a poor farm lad. Hull had been born free, but he knew a few slaves in Stockbridge. Perhaps an independent American nation, founded on liberty and equality, would end slavery and bring equality to all African Americans.

A SOLDIER'S LIFE

General John Paterson took notice of the "intelligent and unusually bright" young man in his company and assigned Hull to be his orderly. Hull stayed behind the battle lines to serve the general's meals, prepare his uniform, tend his horse, and act as a courier, delivering messages to other officers and camps. Hull became a popular personality. "His aptness and wit and his readiness in repartee, as well as the intelligent manner in which he performed all his duties, made him a great favorite with all the officers," Paterson wrote.

Private Hull and the First Stockbridge Company of Berkshire County marched west to the Hudson River Valley in New York State. One group of British troops was moving south from Canada to meet troops coming north from New York City. They hoped to capture the Hudson Valley, cut off New England from the rest of the country, and win the war. The Continental army had other ideas.

The two armies clashed in September near Saratoga, and for a month Hull witnessed several fierce battles that ended with a stunning American victory. For the rest of his life, Hull gleefully told the story of British general "Gentleman Johnny" Burgoyne's humiliating surrender as an American band played "Yankee Doodle."

ON THE MOVE

After the Saratoga campaign, Hull moved south with General Paterson and spent the winter of 1777–78 at Valley Forge with General Washington and his army. The soldiers, starved and half-naked, suffered through a bitter-cold winter. Two thousand of the twelve thousand men died and thousands more deserted. As Paterson's servant, Hull was better clothed and fed than most privates. And he met George Washington, the Marquis de Lafayette, and other officers, including Tadeusz Kościuszko (ko-SHUS-ko), a brilliant young Polish military engineer.

Colonel Kościuszko, who had come from Europe to join the American fight for independence, built forts and bridges for the army and chose the best sites for battle. His work was crucial to the American victory at Saratoga and throughout the rest of the war.

At Kościuszko's request, General Paterson reassigned Hull to be Kościuszko's orderly in 1779. Agrippa Hull found a kindred spirit in Kościuszko, and they shared a quick wit and love of practical jokes. Kościuszko and Hull had more than jokes in common, though: they shared a social conscience.

In Kościuszko's native Poland, poor farmers, called serfs, were virtual slaves of the noblemen, who could buy and sell them. Kościuszko sympathized with the plight of enslaved African Americans and saw that even free blacks like Hull were not treated in the same way as their white countrymen. Though Kościuszko was Hull's superior officer, the two men became close friends.

A DANGEROUS PRANK

One night, Colonel Kościuszko left for a mission that would take him away from camp for several days. As soon as he had gone, Hull organized a party for all the black soldiers. But not just any party. He

dressed up in Kościuszko's Polish army uniform, with a laced coat, sash, sword, and a cap topped with flamboyant ostrich feathers. Since Hull had no officer's boots, he smeared black boot polish on his legs, up to his knees.

Then he broke out the colonel's wine, strutted around the room, "stretched out on the sofa, ordered the servants here and there and bade one of them bring [him] a glass of water." Kościuszko arrived back unexpectedly and stood outside his tent. He watched the partygoers raise their wine glasses to toast Hull's health, calling him "Colonel Kościuszko." When the real colonel burst into the room, the black partygoers fled, and Hull, knowing he was in deep trouble, threw himself at Kościuszko's feet, crying, "Whip me, kill me, Massa; do anything with me, Mr. General."

Instead of punishing him, Kościuszko took his hand, raised him to his feet and said, "Rise, Prince, it is beneath the dignity of an African prince to prostrate himself at the feet of any one." Kościuszko took him to the officers' tent and they all continued to toast Hull as "General Kosciuszko."

If Kościuszko had followed army rules, he would have arrested Hull, who could have gone to prison or received a dishonorable discharge from the army. Instead, Kościuszko went along with the prank.

Hull did not feel humiliated or mocked, for he told this story often. Perhaps he enjoyed making fun of his young mischievous self. Or perhaps he wanted to show the close bond between an aristocratic Polish officer and a poor black private.

GUERILLA WARFARE IN THE SOUTH

Hull accompanied Kościuszko to the south in 1780. When the two men reached North Carolina, they found American troops in a desperate state. Hull suffered through the winter with no blankets, and shoes that were worn through. Food was in short supply as well.

Together, Hull and Kościuszko traveled five thousand grueling miles over the next three years. American and British troops attacked farms and plantations to steal food and livestock and starve the other side into submission. An American general described what Hull saw: "The whole country is in danger of being laid waste by the Whigs [Patriots] and Tories [Loyalists] who pursue each other with as much relentless fury as beasts of prey."

Kościuszko engineered the Continental army's march through rough mountains, ravines, and forests, designing roads and bridges. The two armies fought brief but bloody skirmishes, and Hull helped care for soldiers wounded in battle. He held down men as the surgeons cut off mangled arms and legs with no way to deaden the excruciating pain. Hull never forgot these horrific days.

General Washington's defeat of the British army at Yorktown, Virginia, in 1781 was a major victory for the Americans. But the British army held important seaports in the south, and the two armies, including Colonel Kościuszko and Agrippa Hull, fought on for another eighteen months.

PEACE

The Americans recaptured Charleston, South Carolina, in December 1782, and Kościuszko and Hull sailed together from Charleston to Philadelphia in June 1783. As a token of his gratitude and friendship, Kościuszko gave Hull a valuable Polish flintlock pistol, inlaid with silver and gold. And Kościuszko even offered him more: he asked Agrippa Hull to return to Poland with him as his personal servant and friend.

Hull declined the invitation and watched his dear friend sail away to Europe. His war adventures were over, and Grippy wanted to go home. He walked from Philadelphia to Stockbridge, Massachusetts, in July 1783. He had left home as an unproven, unsophisticated boy of eighteen. He returned a man who had served his country for six years, met heroes of the Revolution, and traveled thousands of miles through the new United States.

Many soldiers, including Agrippa Hull, arrived home with nothing "but poverty in their pockets." But Hull, twenty-four, had served high-ranking army officers. He took a job as butler and handyman for Theodore Sedgwick, a successful Stockbridge lawyer and politician. After only a year, Hull saved enough to buy half an acre of farmland outside the village.

Agrippa Hull met and married Jane Darby, a slave who had run away from her abusive owner in nearby Lenox, Massachusetts. When the owner tried to claim her, Hull appealed to Sedgwick, who helped Jane obtain her freedom. Jane took in boarders to increase the family income, and their family grew to include four children.

Through the years, Hull added to his landholdings until he owned fifteen acres of farm fields and seventy acres of woodland. Though he never became rich, Hull grew wheat, tended a few livestock, planted an apple orchard, and became the most prosperous African American in Stockbridge.

In 1797, fourteen years after he left the army, Agrippa Hull traveled down to New York City to meet Tadeusz Kościuszko, who had returned from Europe. He was surely pleased to hear about Hull's small farm and growing family.

Hull's first wife, Jane, died, and years later he married Margaret (Peggy) Timbroke. They worked together to cater special events, Peggy's root beer and gingerbread being especially popular. "Hull's presence at weddings seemed almost a necessity," wrote Electa Jones, a local historian who knew Hull well. "He wedged himself and his 'good cheer' into every crowded corner, his impromptu rhymes and his courteous jokes . . . always welcome." As for Peggy, she made all the wedding cakes.

Hull's wit could be sharp as well as cheerful, and he was known for "always trimming other men's follies with a keen perception and the biting wit of wisdom." One Sunday after church, Hull and a white man discussed the service. A biracial minister had preached the sermon, and the white man said to Hull, "Well, how do you like nigger preaching?" "Sir," he promptly retorted, "he was half black and half white; I liked my half, how did you like yours?"

According to Electa Jones, Hull "had no cringing servility, and certainly never thought meanly of himself . . . yet he was perfectly free from all airs and show of consequence. He seemed to feel himself every whit a man." When speaking of his race, Hull said, "It is not the cover of the book, but what the book contains [that] is the question. Many a good book has dark covers."

Agrippa Hull had a serious side as well. "He felt deeply the wrongs of his nation," wrote Jones. He had no political power, but he opposed slavery in a personal way. Massachusetts had abolished slavery in 1783, but it lingered on in nearby New York State into the 1820s.

A gradual abolition law had passed in 1799, but slaves born before July 4, 1799, were enslaved for life.

One such woman, Betty Tilden, walked over the New York border through the mountains to Stockbridge with her five-year-old daughter, Mary. Agrippa and Peggy Hull took mother and daughter in, hid them from slave catchers, and later adopted Mary. Hull had been cared for by a loving family when his mother was desperately poor, and he repaid the favor for another child some sixty years later.

AN OLD SOLDIER'S TALES

When he was seventy-two years old, Agrippa Hull traveled to West Point, New York. The United States Military Academy had been established there, and the students had paid for a monument to Tadeusz Kościuszko. A group of Stockbridge citizens traveled to see it, and Hull, "slightly bent by the rheumatism," was "the most noticed and honored of them all." When they clamored to hear Hull's stories about Kościuszko, he began:

> If you wish it, young ladies, you shall have a tale;
> for when it's about the General, love and memory never fail.

At the end of his story, Hull simply said, "He was a lovely man."

The American Revolution gave Agrippa Hull an opportunity to expand his horizons, to fight for a cause he believed in, and to develop the discipline and integrity that served him well all his life. When he told the story of dressing up as Colonel Kościuszko, he always ended on a humble note: "From that day to this, I have never tried to play any part but my own."

CHAPTER THREE

JAMES ARMISTEAD LAFAYETTE

(ca. 1748–1830)

The Yorktown crowd cheered as an elegant carriage rolled down the street. Inside sat the Marquis de Lafayette, a French hero of the Battle of Yorktown. It had been forty-three years since the Continental army, with General Lafayette's help, had defeated the British here in 1781. Now Lafayette was back, hailed as a hero. James Armistead Lafayette, a white-haired black man, cheered along with the rest. He had served under the general at Yorktown, sharing the danger of that month-long siege.

Today, James could see Lafayette waving from his carriage, but he didn't expect the great man to remember him, and certainly not to recognize him. But as Lafayette came near, he stopped his carriage. What happened next was so surprising that the Richmond newspaper reported it: "[Lafayette] called to him by name and took him into his embrace."

A French aristocrat and a poor black farmer met once again as comrades.

In 1781, James, a thirty-three-year-old slave, spent his days working on William Armistead's tobacco plantation in northern Virginia. Marauding bands of British and American soldiers swept through the countryside. Hundreds of enslaved people had run away to freedom with the British army, but James didn't try to escape.

He didn't want to leave home, family, and friends. Instead, he wanted to join George Washington's Continental army. In the northern states, slaves who joined the army were promised freedom after the war. If James enlisted, he thought he might win his freedom, too. William Armistead agreed to let James go. He may have worried that James would run to the British if he refused to let him enlist.

AN ARMY "PIONEER"

In March 1781, James arrived at the camp of the Marquis de Lafayette near Yorktown. The French aristocrat had come to America in 1776 when he was nineteen, eager to join the Americans' fight for liberty and democratic government. By 1781, Lafayette, a major general, commanded his own troops.

African American recruits like James weren't trained as soldiers but worked as "pioneers." They dug trenches, chopped trees to block roads, repaired roads the enemy had destroyed, and built fortifications when the army stayed in one place. Local men like James knew the territory and scoured the region to find food, livestock, horses, and carts for the army. They paid Patriots for the goods they seized, but stole them from the Loyalists.

British army troops stormed through Virginia, raiding farms; burning towns, ships, and warehouses full of tobacco; and seizing weapons. British navy ships patrolled rivers, burning plantations.

The American forces were too few in number to stop them, but a plan was afoot to deal the British a crushing defeat at Yorktown.

SPYING ON THE ENEMY

The British and American armies each had vast networks of spies, and Lafayette ordered James to join their ranks. James had to cross enemy lines, pose as a runaway slave seeking freedom, and offer to serve the British. This was a perfect cover for a spy.

So James worked as a pioneer for the British, scouting and foraging for food, and reported what he learned to Lafayette through a relay team of spies. James couldn't read or write, so he whispered his information to another trusted spy who sneaked across American lines to deliver the message to General Lafayette.

IN THE GENERAL'S TENT

Then a stroke of luck. General Lord Cornwallis, commander of the British troops, assigned James to be a waiter at his table. Now James was in a better position to find out what Cornwallis and his generals were planning.

Lafayette reported to Washington, "A correspondent of mine servant to Lord Cornwallis . . . says [the British] are still in town but expect to move." James couldn't discover

> ## "HIS INTELLIGENCES FROM THE ENEMY'S CAMP WERE INDUSTRIOUSLY COLLECTED AND MORE FAITHFULLY DELIVER'D."
>
> —*Marquis de Lafayette*

where, though. Lafayette continued, "His Lordship [Cornwallis] is so shy [careful] of his papers that my honest friend says he cannot get at them."

But James, his "honest friend," stood near while Cornwallis talked with his officers. James moved forward to serve food and drink to the men, then retreated into the corner. The officers probably didn't even notice him, or if they did, they assumed he couldn't understand their military talk. But James listened and understood, and a few hours later Lafayette learned what James had heard.

In late July, Cornwallis set up a base camp in Yorktown. Then another brilliant stroke of luck. James had proved such a "loyal" servant that Cornwallis asked him to spy on the Americans. So James became a double agent—spying on the British for the Americans, and pretending to spy on the Americans for the British. He traveled back and forth between the two armies. British sentries had orders to let him leave and reenter their lines. American sentries knew him and let him pass.

DOUBLE AGENT

James told Lafayette all he knew of Cornwallis's plans. But he told Cornwallis only what Lafayette wanted the British general to hear— false troop locations and inflated troop numbers. One day, James delivered a crumpled letter to Cornwallis that he claimed he had found on the road. It was a letter from Lafayette to an American general discussing a large number of American troops coming to reinforce his men. These troops did not exist, but Cornwallis never knew that, so he didn't attack Lafayette, thinking he would be outnumbered. He believed that James was a loyal British spy.

In mid-August, Washington and French lieutenant general Rochambeau marched their army of seven thousand French and American soldiers from New York to Virginia. In early September, French ships arrived with more soldiers to support Lafayette and Washington. Cornwallis was surrounded on land, and French ships blocked his escape by sea. As Washington built fortifications and prepared for battle, James continued sending reports to Lafayette: Cornwallis had run out of fodder for his horses and was forced to slaughter them all. Smallpox broke out in his camp and many people died. Cornwallis had begged for reinforcements from British headquarters in New York City, but they didn't arrive.

VICTORY

On September 28, the combined American and French troops began a siege of the British forces at Yorktown. They bombarded them with cannon fire, moving their troops closer to enemy lines day by day. Cut off from food, supplies, and military help, his army starving, Cornwallis surrendered on October 17, 1781, while James slipped away to the American camp one last time. American general Nathanael Greene commented, "We have been beating the bush and the General [Washington] has come to catch the bird."

A few days later, General Cornwallis paid a courtesy visit to General Lafayette. As Cornwallis entered Lafayette's tent, there stood James, his personal servant, his "loyal" spy, standing behind General Lafayette. James was dressed in the uniform of the Continental army! He had played a dangerous game—and won.

STILL ENSLAVED

After the war, the United States of America gained its independence, but James did not. He was forced to return to Armistead's plantation. The Continental army had promised freedom to slaves who had served as soldiers, but James had been a spy, not a soldier. He was still enslaved, but he was determined to change that.

Under Virginia law, owners could not free a slave, except by a special act passed by the Virginia Assembly. Because James was illiterate,

"A MOST EARNEST DESIRE OF GAINING THAT LIBERTY WHICH IS SO DEAR TO ALL MANKIND."

he would have needed help to prepare his petition. "Being impelled by a most earnest desire of gaining that liberty which is so dear to all mankind," the appeal described his activities at Yorktown, "praying that an act may pass for his emancipation."

To strengthen his case, James got word to Lafayette, who was visiting George Washington. Lafayette bitterly opposed slavery and tried for years to convince Washington to support the cause of abolition. When Washington refused, Lafayette declared, "I would never have drawn my sword in the cause of America, if I could have conceived that thereby I was founding a land of slavery."

Lafayette sent a glowing letter praising James's service, and James sent it to the legislature.

This is to Certify that the Bearer By the Name of James has done Essential Services to me While I had the Honour to Command in this State. His intelligences from the Enemy's Camp were Industriously Collected and More faithfully deliver'd. He properly Acquitted Himself with Some important Commissions I Gave Him and Appears to me Entitled to Every Reward his Situation Can Admit of. Done Under my Hand, Richmond November 21st, 1784

—Lafayette

STILL WAITING

Two years passed and nothing happened. The assembly had either lost his petition or ignored it. So James sent another one in November 1786, using stronger arguments. James's first appeal had been an emotional one, asking for "that liberty which is so dear to all mankind."

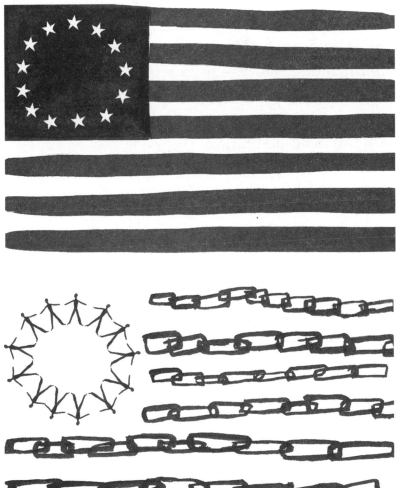

His second petition turned political, claiming that he deserved "the just right which all mankind have to Freedom."

Despite "his own state of bondage," he had volunteered from "an honest desire to serve this country . . . during the ravages of Lord Cornwallis thro' this state." His spying activities had put him "often at the peril of his life" and he "humbly intreats that he may be granted those Freedoms, which he flatters himself he has in Some degree contributed to establish." James boldly claimed a bit of credit for winning the war.

Finally, in January 1787, the assembly granted James his freedom and paid William Armistead the market price for a man like James. They paid James nothing for his war service (since he was not a soldier) or for his lifetime of work for Armistead. He did receive forty acres of land near the Armistead plantation.

LIFE IN FREEDOM

As a freeman, James chose new names for himself. He took Armistead as a middle name, but he gave to himself and his family the name of his hero. He became James Armistead Lafayette. For the rest of his life, he farmed his land in Virginia with his wife and family. But freedom and a farm didn't bring prosperity. In 1816, local tax records described his land as "broken, and much worn."

Two years later, when he was nearly seventy, James appealed to the Virginia Assembly again, stating he was unable to support himself. He asked for a soldier's pension and received $60 in cash and a promise of $40 a year for the rest of his life. This was the pension given to army privates who served in the Revolution.

Twice a year, James Armistead Lafayette traveled to Richmond to receive his $20 pension payment from James Heath, a state employee.

The former spy must have told his war stories to Heath, for when Heath later wrote a romance adventure novel of the Revolution titled *Edge-Hill*, he included a slave called James, who served as a spy for Lafayette.

And it may have been Lafayette who arranged for James to have his portrait painted in 1824, after the two men met at the parade in Yorktown. John B. Martin, a well-known artist, portrayed a handsome man, white-haired now, proudly gazing forward, loyal to his country, dressed in the uniform of the Continental army.

PART TWO

SLAVES IN THE CRADLE OF LIBERTY

Massachusetts settlers had owned slaves since the colony's beginnings in the 1630s. Their ships carried captives from Africa, and auctioneers sold them on the streets of Boston. New England shipowners and merchants made fortunes working in the slave trade.

No laws were ever passed to make slavery legal in Massachusetts, but no law made it illegal either. During the seventeenth and eighteenth centuries, various laws and customs controlled slaves' lives. On Sundays, they could attend church, but they had to sit in the African section. They had a 9 o'clock curfew every night and could not gather in groups at any hour. Owners were afraid of "unruly behavior" or worse: violence or insurrection.

In 1776, more than five thousand enslaved African Americans made up 2 percent of Massachusetts' population. Half of them lived in or near Boston. Women worked as household servants and men often learned skilled trades. Most Massachusetts slaveholders owned just one or two slaves, so northern slaves could not count on the close community of slaves in the south, where large numbers lived together.

Free and enslaved African Americans in Massachusetts did have some rights. They could bring lawsuits in court, learn to read, marry, and receive a jury trial. But they couldn't serve on juries or vote. And slaves were bound to their owners for life.

THE CLAMOR FOR FREEDOM

African Americans in Boston heard the shouts about natural rights that sounded during the 1760s as the town became the center of radical thought in the colonies. They heard about petitions that Patriots sent to lawmakers—and they began to do the same thing. During the 1770s, African Americans, free and enslaved, sent petitions against slavery and inequality to the Massachusetts Assembly using the same language of liberty and equality that white men used.

Both Phillis Wheatley and Prince Hall listened closely to the language of liberty. Both arrived in Boston on slave ships when they were young. Both eventually gained their freedom. Both supported American independence and declared that independence should extend to all African Americans.

Wheatley, the first African American woman to publish her poetry, used her celebrity to speak out against slavery. Hall, an early leader of nonviolent protest, organized his people to work for the abolition of slavery and education for their children. Elizabeth Freeman lived far from the clamor in Boston. She couldn't read or write. But she fought her way to freedom through the courts and helped to emancipate thousands more Massachusetts slaves.

Wheatley, Hall, and Freeman agreed with white Boston Patriots that liberty is everyone's birthright—and these three took action to bring it about.

CHAPTER FOUR

PHILLIS WHEATLEY

(ca. 1753–1784)

There she sat in the stately meeting room in Boston, a frail black girl, small for her eighteen years, surrounded by a group of formidable men. The royal governor of Massachusetts and his lieutenant governor were there, along with seven church ministers, three poets, and a few rich merchants. They were the political, spiritual, and business leaders of the colony, many of them graduates of Harvard College.

These men didn't agree on politics. A half dozen were staunch Loyalists; others, like John Hancock, led Patriot protests. But the group of eighteen did agree to interview Phillis Wheatley to decide if she really wrote the poems she said she did. Many people thought that Africans weren't intelligent or imaginative enough to write poems. So the leading men of Boston met to settle the matter, at least in Phillis's case.

We don't know exactly what they asked her. Perhaps they gave her a quiz on the important English poets of the day, such as Alexander Pope, her favorite. Or questioned her about Greek and Roman gods and heroes who appear in many of her poems. The ministers may have tested her on Bible verses, for many of Wheatley's poems carry a religious message. They might have set her a topic and asked her to write a poem then and there, as a gentleman once did in Phillis's parlor. Whatever it was that her examiners asked her to do, she did it well.

At the end of the day, they all signed a statement to "assure the World, that the Poems specified in the following [book] were (as we verily believe) written by Phillis, a young Negro Girl, who was but a few Years since, brought an uncultivated Barbarian from *Africa*. . . . She has been examined by some of the best Judges, and is thought qualified to write them."

Was Phillis Wheatley insulted by her examination or proud to show off her knowledge? Probably a bit of both.

Eleven years earlier, in 1761, Phillis had stood shivering with fright before a small crowd on the dock in Boston. She heard a white man, the slave auctioneer, shout words that she could not understand. One by one, the African men and women around her walked away with their new owners.

John Wheatley, a wealthy tailor, merchant, and shipowner, had come to the auction with his wife, Susanna. Their household slaves were getting on in years, and Susanna, growing old herself, wanted a strong woman to do the housework.

Instead, the Wheatleys came home with a sickly child, wrapped only in a ragged bit of rug. Compassion, not common sense, caused Susanna to buy the seven-year-old who would need more help than she could possibly give, at least for a few years.

Susanna named her Phillis, after the slave ship that brought her from Africa. Phillis lived in the Wheatleys' elegant home in the middle of Boston, not in the carriage house with the other family slaves.

"I WAS A POOR LITTLE OUTCAST & STRANGER WHEN SHE TOOK ME IN."

Susanna and her teenage daughter, Mary, nursed Phillis back to health, and the girl's intellect began to blossom.

In a little more than a year, with Mary as her teacher, Phillis learned to speak English and read even the most difficult parts of the Bible. Soon she was reading classic English writers and studying astronomy, Latin, history, and geography.

Phillis had found a home and a loving foster mother in Susanna Wheatley. She wrote, "I was a poor little outcast & stranger when she took me in, not only into her house but I presently became, a sharer in her most tender affections, I was treated by her more like her child than her Servant."

Phillis learned the social graces of a young white lady, but she knew that not everyone would treat her as well as the Wheatleys did. At home, Phillis ate at their dining table. When she dined at other Boston homes, she asked to eat alone at a table nearby. She knew her place in Boston society. When Phillis attended church, she sat in the balcony with the slaves.

No one could teach Phillis Wheatley how to balance her two worlds—polite white society and her African heritage—for no one shared her position. But Phillis learned how to do it—with poetry. What's more, she used poetry to speak about the fractious politics of the day.

A PASSION FOR POETRY

Phillis began to write poetry around age twelve. "Her own curiosity led her to it," John Wheatley, her master, wrote. Writing was a common hobby among educated men and women, but usually only men's poems appeared in newspapers or pamphlets. That didn't stop Phillis. Susanna Wheatley made sure that Phillis always had a candle beside her bed and a warm fire in winter so that if she woke in the night with an inspired line, she could light her candle and write "without rising or taking cold, [to] secure the swift-winged fancy, ere it fled."

"HER OWN CURIOSITY LED HER TO IT."

Susanna also acted as Phillis's literary agent, sending one of her early poems to a Newport, Rhode Island, newspaper. Two dinner guests at the Wheatleys had told their story of nearly drowning at sea, and Phillis wrote: "Did Fear and Danger so perplex your Mind, / As made you fearful of the Whistling Wind?"

Phillis wrote about real people and events. She wrote poems called elegies when people died. She wrote to praise famous men. She addressed a poem to Harvard College students, chiding them for partying too much. She mentioned gods and mythic figures from ancient Greece and Rome, but her message was most often religious. When she was fourteen, she wrote a poem, "On Being Brought from Africa to America," that is often reprinted.

'Twas mercy brought me from my Pagan land,
Taught my benighted soul to understand
That there's a God, that there's a Saviour too:
Once I redemption neither sought nor knew.
Some view our sable race with scornful eye,
"Their colour is a diabolic die."
Remember, Christians, Negros, *black as* Cain,
May be refin'd, and join th' angelic train.

This poem has been attacked by modern critics as a betrayal of her African heritage and a justification for slavery. There is more to the poem, though. Phillis is saying that religion is most important in her life, and she insists that blacks and whites are equal in the sight of her God. Phillis's devout Christian faith was acceptable to her readers, but her pride in being African was a radical notion. At fourteen, she had the courage to express it publicly.

POETRY AND POLITICS

The year Phillis wrote that poem, 1768, British army troops occupied Boston to quell protests against harsh regulations on taxes and trade. Two years later, Phillis described the Boston Massacre, where several Americans, including Crispus Attucks, half Native American and half African American, died in a confrontation with British soldiers. Her poem was published in the *Boston Evening-Post* a week after the event.

> from *On the Affray in King Street,*
> *on the Evening of the 5th of March, 1770*
>
> *Long as in* Freedom's *Cause the wise contend,*
> *Dear to your unity shall Fame extend;*
> *While to the World, the letter's Stone shall tell,*
> *How* Caldwell, Attucks, Gray *and Mav'rick fell.*

American Patriots continued to demand more freedom to govern themselves. Phillis Wheatley read the newspapers, saw the protests, and added her voice to the clamor, proudly calling herself "Afric's muse" or "Ethiop" in many poems.

In 1772, she and other Patriots thought that the appointment of Lord Dartmouth as secretary of state for North America would improve relations between Britain and the colonies. She wrote a poem to Dartmouth, expressing her hope in extravagant verse.

Hail, happy day, when smiling like the morn,
Fair Freedom *rose* New-England *to adorn:*
The northern clime beneath her genial ray,
Dartmouth, *congratulates thy blissful sway.*
. . . .
No more, America, *in mournful strain*
Of wrongs, and grievance unredress'd complain,
No longer shall thou dread the iron chain,
Which wanton Tyranny with lawless hand
Had made, and with it meant t' enslave the land.

She had heard Patriots talk of British "slavery" as a metaphor. But she wrote about the pain of actual slavery.

I, young in life, by seeming cruel fate
Was snatch'd from Afric's fancy'd happy seat:
What pangs excruciating must molest,
What sorrows labour in my parent's breast?
. . . .
Such, such my case. And can I then but pray
Others may never feel tyrannic sway?

FINDING A FRIEND

As more of Wheatley's poems appeared in print in New England, New York, and Philadelphia, she became the most famous African American of her day. But, despite her fame, she must have felt lonely. In Boston drawing rooms, no other faces were like hers, unless they served tea and cakes. She did find one friend in Newport, Rhode Island. Obour Tanner, an enslaved African American woman, "very dark, pious, sensible, intelligent, and respected," corresponded with Phillis for many years.

> ### "I HOPE THE CORRESPONDENCE BETWEEN US WILL CONTINUE . . . WHICH . . . I HOPE MAY HAVE THE HAPPY EFFECT OF IMPROVING OUR MUTUAL FRIENDSHIP."
>
> —*Phillis Wheatley, to Obour Tanner*

Their letters often read like church sermons. Phillis wrote: "Till we meet in the regions of consummate blessedness, let us endeavor by the assistance of divine grace, to live the life, and we Shall die the death of the Righteous." We can also hear the whisper of personal affection from Phillis: "I recd. last evening your kind & friendly Letter, and am <u>not</u> a little animated thereby."

POEMS ON VARIOUS SUBJECTS, RELIGIOUS AND MORAL

As Phillis's collection of poems grew, she wanted to publish a book. In her day, books were often published after enough readers subscribed and paid in advance for the printing costs. Susanna Wheatley advertised in a Boston newspaper for subscribers but didn't receive enough orders.

However, Phillis had admirers across the ocean in London, who had read her poems in English newspapers. One of them, the Countess of Huntingdon, agreed to print Phillis's book. But first, to prove to a skeptical public that an enslaved African female could write such poems, Phillis took her examination with Boston's educated elite. Phillis Wheatley's book of poems contained the following statement from the Boston leaders.

> WE whose Names are under-written, do assure the World,
> that the Poems specified in the following Page, were (as we
> verily believe) written by Phillis, a young Negro Girl, who was
> but a few Years since, brought an uncultivated Barbarian
> from Africa, and has ever since been, and now is, under the
> Disadvantage of serving as a Slave in a Family in this Town.
> She has been examined by some of the best Judges, and is
> thought qualified to write them.

The countess knew how curious the public would be about the author and paid an artist to draw a portrait of Phillis. The Wheatleys chose Scipio Moorhead, another enslaved Bostonian. His drawing of Phillis, engraved in London and printed in her book, shows a thoughtful young woman, quill pen in hand, book at her elbow, thinking of her next poem. Phillis thanked Moorhead in a poem, "To S. M. a Young African Painter, on Seeing His Works."

> When first thy pencil did those beauties give,
> And breathing figures learnt from thee to live,
> How did those prospects give my soul delight,
> A new creation rushing on my sight?
> . . . .

Still may the painter's and the poet's fire
To aid thy pencil, and thy verse conspire!

In May 1773, Phillis sailed to England with the Wheatleys' son to promote her forthcoming book. She had been in poor health, suffering from asthma, and the doctor thought sea air would do her good. Evidently it did, for she entered a social whirlwind when she reached London.

A LONDON CELEBRITY

Phillis became as popular abroad as she was in Boston. London was quite a different place, though. This city of eight hundred thousand people was the center of the British Empire, the home of lords and ladies who were far grander than Boston's small-town elite. Twenty-year-old Phillis, intelligent, poised, and articulate, impressed all who met her.

The Lord Mayor of London gave her a valuable copy of *Paradise Lost* by John Milton. The Earl of Dartmouth and several lords and ladies received her in their drawing rooms, and Benjamin Franklin came to call. Wheatley wrote to Obour Tanner: "The Friends I found there among the Nobility and Gentry. Their Benevolent conduct towards me . . . fills me with astonishment, I can scarcely Realize it."

> "THE FRIENDS I FOUND THERE AMONG THE NOBILITY AND GENTRY. THEIR BENEVOLENT CONDUCT TOWARDS ME . . . FILLS ME WITH ASTONISHMENT, I CAN SCARCELY REALIZE IT."

She loved being a tourist. She marveled at the lions, tigers, and crown jewels at the Tower of London. She was awestruck by stately Westminster Abbey and the treasures in the British Museum. She attended the theater (forbidden in Boston), the Royal Greenwich Observatory, and "too many things & Places to trouble you with in a Letter," she wrote.

At last, in September 1773, her book was published.

POEMS ON VARIOUS SUBJECTS, RELIGIOUS AND MORAL,
by Phillis Wheatley, Negro Servant to Mr. John Wheatley,
of Boston, in New England.

Servant, not *slave*, was the word used in polite society.

Unfortunately, Phillis was not in London when the book came out, and she left England before she had a chance to meet her patron, the Countess of Huntingdon, as well as King George III. Phillis had received news that Susanna Wheatley was very ill, and Phillis took the next ship back to Boston. Her mistress meant more to her than the king of England. Several months later, when Mrs. Wheatley passed away, Phillis wrote to Obour Tanner: "I have lately met with a great trial in the death of my mistress, let us imagine the loss of a Parent, Sister or Brother the tenderness of all these were united, in her."

> **"I AM NOW UPON MY OWN FOOTING AND WHATEVER I GET BY [BOOK SALES] IS ENTIRELY MINE, & IT IS THE CHIEF I HAVE TO DEPEND UPON."**

THE PRICE OF FREEDOM

John Wheatley finally gave Phillis her freedom in 1773. She continued to live in the Wheatley home, but she now had to earn money for her future. She gave readings to ladies' groups in Boston, and she asked friends and acquaintances to help her sell her books.

In a letter to a customs officer in Connecticut, she wrote:

> *I beg the favour that you would honour the enclos'd Proposals [books], & use your interest with Gentlemen & Ladies of your acquaintance to subscribe also, for the more subscribers there are, the more it will be for my advantage as I am to have half [the money from] the sale of the Books, This I am the more solicitous for, as I am now upon my own footing and whatever I get by [book sales] is entirely mine, & it is the Chief I have to depend upon.*

As Phillis sold her books in Boston parlors, Britain sent more troops and closed the port of Boston to all trade. The Patriots threatened to go to war to defend their freedom. Phillis wrote to Samson Occom, a Native American Christian minister:

> *In every human Breast, God has implanted a Principle, which we call Love of Freedom; it is impatient of Oppression, and pants for Deliverance. . . . I will assert, that the same Principle lives in us [people of color]. God grant Deliverance in his own Way and Time, and get him honour upon all those whose Avarice [greed] impels them to countenance and help forward the Calamities of their fellow Creatures.*

This was Phillis Wheatley's strongest outcry against slavery. She called for God's punishment on slave traders, who grew rich from "the Calamities of their fellow Creatures." She went on to denounce "the strange Absurdity of their Conduct whose Words and Actions are so diametrically opposite. How well the Cry for Liberty, and the reverse Disposition for the exercise of oppressive Power over others agree—I humbly think it does not require the Penetration of a Philosopher to determine." This is an attack on those Patriots who cried for freedom, yet kept African Americans enslaved.

Wheatley's earlier poems had expressed pity for slaves; now she heaped scorn on slave owners. Her letter to Occom appeared in newspapers throughout Massachusetts and Connecticut.

In the mid-1770s, when the war with Britain had just begun, Phillis wrote to

"IN EVERY HUMAN BREAST, GOD HAS IMPLANTED A PRINCIPLE, WHICH WE CALL LOVE OF FREEDOM."

Obour Tanner: "Possibly the Ambition & Thirst of Dominion in some, is design'd as the punishment of the national vices of others." But whose "Ambition and Thirst for Dominion?" Great Britain had tried to maintain "Dominion" over rebellious Americans. Americans had "Dominion" over five hundred thousand slaves and were "thirsting" for more as their ships sailed back and forth across the Atlantic, filled with captives.

Phillis went on: "Let us leave the Event to him whose wisdom alone can bring good out of Evil." God will right the wrong of slavery. But even her pious Christian attitude contained a sting as she rebuked the "craftiness of the enemies of this seemingly devoted Country." Britain was "crafty" while America only *seemed* to be a Christian country.

VISITING GENERAL WASHINGTON

When George Washington came to Massachusetts to build the Continental army, twenty-two-year-old Phillis Wheatley, who once sat at a separate table in Boston's parlors, now dared to approach the most powerful man in America. She had written a poem for him and sent it to him with a letter introducing herself.

Washington responded and wrote: "I thank you most sincerely for your polite notice of me, in the elegant Lines you enclosed." He praised her "great poetical Talents" and wanted to publish the poem "to give the World this new instance of your genius," but he might be thought vain if he did so.

Washington invited Phillis to visit him at his headquarters, and she accepted. No one wrote down their conversation, but after the visit, Washington gave her poem to an officer, who had it printed in Philadelphia and Virginia.

from *To His Excellency George Washington*

Thee, first in place and honours,—we demand
The grace and glory of thy martial band.
Fam'd for thy valour, for thy virtues more,
Hear every tongue thy guardian aid implore!
. . . .
Proceed, great chief, with virtue on thy side,
Thy ev'ry action let the goddess guide.
A crown, a mansion, and a throne that shine,
With gold unfading, WASHINGTON! be thine.

MARRIED LIFE

John Wheatley died in March 1778, and his daughter, Mary Wheatley, died a few months later. Now Phillis was alone. In November 1778, she agreed to marry John Peters, a free black man. Did she marry for love or security? We can only guess.

Phillis's friend Obour Tanner knew John Peters and didn't approve of the match. She wrote: "Poor Phillis let herself down by marrying; yes ma'am." The couple moved to a village outside Boston, where Peters started a grocery business that failed. Their first two babies died. Phillis wrote to Obour:

> *Tho' I have been silent, I have not been unmindful of you*
> *but a variety of hindrances was the cause of my not writing*
> *to you—But in time to Come I hope our correspondence*
> *will revive—and revive in better times.—Pray write me*
> *soon for I long to hear from you—you may depend on*
> *constant replies.*

Despite all her struggles and sorrow, Phillis continued to write poetry. In 1779, during the American Revolution, she advertised for subscribers for a second book but failed to get enough. London, where her first book was launched, was now enemy territory.

In 1784, when the war was over, Phillis published *Liberty and Peace* as a four-page pamphlet. She aimed a final jab at Britain and its "savage Troops" and predicted a happy future for her country: "To every Realm shall *Peace* her Charms display, / And Heavenly *Freedom* spread her golden Ray."

No "golden Ray" fell on Phillis, though. In desperate circumstances, she tried again to gather subscribers for her second book, and again she failed. Peters was in and out of debtor's prison, and Phillis lived with her third infant in a squalid boardinghouse, working as a housemaid. In September, *Boston Magazine* published her poem titled "To

Mr. and Mrs. ——, on the Death of their Infant Son," a subject she knew only too well.

> So sweetly blooming once that lovely boy,
> His father's hope, his mother's only joy,
> Nor charms nor innocence prevail to save,
> From the grim monarch of the gloomy grave!

Three months later, Phillis and her third infant died—on the same day. A sad group of friends followed their coffin to an unmarked grave. John Peters was not there.

Eventually, he did show up to claim her few belongings. He sold them all to pay his debts, including her copy of *Paradise Lost*, the gift from the Lord Mayor of London. Peters also retrieved the manuscript for her second collection of poems, but the book was never published and the poems have been lost.

Phillis Wheatley's story had a terrible ending—a husband who couldn't support her, three children dead, and dying in poverty at age thirty-one. Yet she had been educated and loved by the Wheatleys. She had been celebrated as a poet. She dared to add her voice to the American Patriots calling for freedom. And she demanded more: freedom for her people who were enslaved.

If she had been healthier, if she had lived in a time of peace, if her husband had provided for her, if she had had more practical skills to support herself and her children, perhaps her story would have ended differently. Despite everything, Phillis Wheatley dared to speak her truth to the world: she was proud to be a poet, a Christian, and an African American.

CHAPTER FIVE

ELIZABETH "MUMBET" FREEMAN

(ca. 1742–1829)

This morning, just like every morning, Mumbet teased a blazing fire from the coals in the kitchen fireplace. In the quiet of dawn, she thought about the recent meeting in the Sheffield, Massachusetts, town hall.

People had crowded in to hear a reading of the new state constitution. It laid out the system of government and the principles behind that government: *All men are born free and equal and have certain natural, essential, and unalienable rights.* Mumbet didn't understand all the words, but she understood "free and equal," because she wasn't. Mumbet was enslaved.

When she finished her morning chores, she began walking the three miles from the Ashley farm to the village of Sheffield. She passed farmhouses where farmers and hired hands lived. Farmhands could choose to leave a cruel master; Mumbet had no such choice. At the junction near the village, she crossed the road and walked toward a lawyer's office. She was on a quest for her freedom.

Mumbet, born enslaved around 1742 in the Hudson Valley of New York, grew up speaking Dutch. When she was about fourteen, her owner died and left her to his daughter Hannah, who had married Colonel John Ashley. Perhaps it was then that Mumbet was torn from her parents and sent to Massachusetts, where people spoke English, a foreign language to her. She carried gifts from her parents that she kept all her life: a long black dress from her father and a short gown from her mother. These weren't fine clothes, but they were precious links to her childhood.

Mumbet's new home in Sheffield was owned by John Ashley, the richest man in town. He lived with Hannah, their three daughters, and one son. Ashley's four enslaved men lived in a room in the barn, and Mumbet lived in a small room next to the kitchen. When Mumbet gave birth to a daughter, Lizzy, she shared the room with her mother.

The Ashley women worked alongside Mumbet, cooking, spinning, and sewing. But the heavy work—doing laundry, making soap, and scrubbing floors—was left to Mumbet. She didn't mind hard work, but Hannah Ashley's sharp tongue was harder to bear. Hannah was called "a shrew untameable" and "the most despotic of mistresses." Hannah tested Mumbet's good nature every single day.

"JUST TO STAND ONE MINUTE ON GOD'S *AIRTH* A FREE WOMAN."

WAITING AND WATCHING

One day, Mumbet was making bread, as she did each week. She mixed and kneaded the dough and shoveled hot coals into the brick oven built in the fireplace. When the bread had risen, Mumbet shoveled out the coals and placed the bread in the oven to bake. Lizzy mixed pieces of leftover dough to make her own little loaf of bread.

Just then, Hannah Ashley entered the room and screamed at the girl. "Thief!" She raised the hot coal shovel and swung it at Lizzy. Mumbet's arm shot out to take the blow, which cut to the bone. The wound was slow to heal, but she refused to cover it.

"I had a bad arm all winter, but Madam had the worst of it," Mumbet said. "I never covered the wound, and when people said to me, before Madam,—'Why, Betty! what ails your arm?' I only answered—'ask missis.'"

Hannah Ashley couldn't break the woman's spirit, but slavery weighed heavily on Mumbet. She said, "Any time, any time while I was a slave, if one minute's freedom had been offered to me, and I had been told I must die at the end of that minute, I would have taken it—just to stand one minute on God's *airth* a free woman—I would."

BIRTH OF A REVOLUTION

Ideas of freedom were stirring in Colonel Ashley's world as well. In the 1760s, people in Boston protested against new British taxes on American colonists who had been governing—and taxing—themselves for 150 years. Echoes of the uproar reached quiet Sheffield, but Colonel Ashley and his friends were conservative country landowners, not Boston radicals. When revolutionary talk spread throughout the colonies, they were finally convinced.

The town's leaders gathered in Colonel Ashley's study in January 1773. Mumbet heard them argue about the issues as she served them food and drink. At the end of all their talk, an ambitious young lawyer named Theodore Sedgwick wrote down their declaration to send to Boston. Mumbet couldn't read the Sheffield Resolves but she understood the words:

RESOLVED, That mankind in a state of nature are equal,
free, and independent of each other, and have a right to the
undisturbed enjoyment of their lives, their liberty and property.

Mumbet had no property, except the clothes on her back and those her parents had given her. She had no liberty either, but she certainly longed for it.

The Resolves went on:

Resolved, That the great end of political society is to secure in a
more effectual manner those rights and privileges wherewith God
and nature have made us free.

Did Colonel Ashley and the others believe that Mumbet had the right to be free? Would their "political society"—the government—help her secure her rights? The radical ideas in the Sheffield Resolves were just words, not law. So Mumbet watched and waited.

She watched as Massachusetts joined the twelve other American colonies and declared independence from Britain in 1776. She watched local Sheffield men go off to war to secure that independence. She waited until Massachusetts wrote a constitution in 1780, and she went to town to hear it read.

Article I. All men are born free and equal, and have certain
natural, essential, and unalienable rights; among which may
be reckoned the right of enjoying and defending their lives and
liberties; that of acquiring, possessing, and protecting property; in
fine, that of seeking and obtaining their safety and happiness.

Mumbet knew her waiting was over. Those grand ideas of Colonel Ashley's and his friends were now the law. Would she dare to test them? She would. She walked into the office of Theodore Sedgwick, the young lawyer who wrote down the Sheffield Resolves.

"Sir," said she, "I heard that paper read yesterday that says, 'all men are born equal,' and that every man has a right to freedom. I am not a dumb *critter*; won't the law give me my freedom?"

Sedgwick was not rich and powerful like John Ashley. Would he dare to oppose Ashley in court?

He would.

"I AM NOT A DUMB CRITTER; WON'T THE LAW GIVE ME MY FREEDOM?"

Because Mumbet was a woman, Sedgwick wanted to strengthen his case by adding Brom, a male slave owned by Ashley, to the lawsuit.

FREEDOM ON TRIAL

First, the county court sent to Colonel Ashley a notice called a writ of replevin, demanding that he release his "property." He refused. The court sent another writ, and again he refused. Then the court summoned him to appear, and on August 21, 1781, Mumbet faced her owner in the courtroom. If she won, she would be free. If she lost, her life could be harder than ever.

There is no record of what the lawyers said at her trial. But the jury, all white men, were convinced by Mumbet's lawyers, and the judge ruled that Mumbet and Brom were free. Not only that, Colonel Ashley also was required to pay the two freed slaves thirty shillings for their long years of labor. Small though this amount was, it recognized people's right to be paid for their work.

Before Mumbet's case, other Massachusetts slaves had sued for their freedom. They had been promised freedom by owners who then broke that promise. Or they were beaten and took their masters to court for assault. But the Ashleys had made no promise of freedom, and Mumbet did not prosecute Mrs. Ashley for the beating she gave Mumbet. It was slavery itself that Mumbet challenged— and she won.

Other Massachusetts judges accepted the verdict in her case, and two years after Mumbet's trial, a judge decreed that slavery was unconstitutional in Massachusetts. Seven years later, the 1790 state census recorded slaves—0.

Mumbet had helped to free her daughter, too, and more than five thousand people.

After the 1781 trial, Brom disappeared from history, but Catharine Sedgwick, Theodore's daughter, wrote a memoir that included many stories about Mumbet. In one of her first acts as a free woman, she returned to the courthouse to give herself a new name: Elizabeth Freeman. She left the Ashleys and set forth "seeking and obtaining her safety and happiness."

LIVING FREE

Freeman went to work for her lawyer, Theodore Sedgwick, in nearby Stockbridge. Though she was hired as a housekeeper, for the next twenty-seven years she became much more. Mrs. Sedgwick suffered from severe depression, and Freeman nursed her, comforting her better than anyone else could. In addition, Freeman became a second mother to the seven Sedgwick children and worked as a midwife, delivering babies in the town. Freeman's nurturing skills were widely known, but it took an armed rebellion in 1786 to bring forth her iron will and nerves of steel.

Farmers in western Massachusetts armed themselves and fought against the lawyers and judges who were taking away their farms when they couldn't pay their debts. Theodore Sedgwick became a target of their attacks. In late February 1787, he was in Boston on business and his family fled from Stockbridge. They left Freeman alone to guard their home. She gathered the Sedgwick silver and jewelry and hid it inside her own trunk, under her dresses and petticoats.

When armed marauders banged at the door, Freeman let them in, to stop them from destroying the house. They ransacked the place, searching for Sedgwick, jabbing their bayonets under the beds and into the closets. When they couldn't find Sedgwick, they searched the cellar and found a supply of liquor. Freeman gave them some of the worst-tasting beer, which they spat out. Then they climbed to the attic and found Freeman's trunk, secured with a padlock.

They demanded the key from her.

She refused.

They hurled racial insults at her.

She replied that if they wanted to rob a poor Negro woman's trunk, they would have to break it open. They left her trunk alone—with all the Sedgwick valuables inside. An unarmed woman foiled these men who had terrorized whole towns.

In 1807, when Mrs. Sedgwick died and the children were grown, Freeman retired. She had saved enough money to buy a small house and a few acres of land in the hills outside Stockbridge. Her daughter, Lizzy, had children, and they had children—Freeman's grandchildren and great-grandchildren. Freeman lived among them for the rest of her life.

Catharine Sedgwick, who wrote down some of her memories of Elizabeth "Mumbet" Freeman, also wrote a touching epitaph for Freeman's tombstone in the Sedgwick family plot.

Elizabeth Freeman
(known by the name of Mum-Bett)
Died Dec. 28th 1829.
Her supposed age was 85 years.

She was born a slave and remained a slave for nearly
thirty years. She could neither read nor write; yet in her
own sphere she had no superior nor equal. . . . She never
violated a truth, nor failed to perform a duty. In every
situation of domestic trial she was the most efficient helper
and the tenderest friend. Good mother, farewell!

Though Freeman lived far from Boston, she understood the principles that fired up the revolutionaries. Acting on those principles, she managed to free herself and thousands more and set about seeking her happiness, just as the Massachusetts constitution had decreed.

CHAPTER SIX

PRINCE HALL

(ca. 1735–1807)

On a late winter's day in 1775, Prince Hall made his way through the crowded lanes of Boston. He moved cautiously, for he was going to meet a British soldier, an enemy who occupied the city.

Boston had become a powder keg of rebellion. The Sons of Liberty fought in the streets against British troops, and Patriot mobs tarred and feathered American Loyalists, who sided with Britain. Hall supported a cause that most white people—Patriot or Loyalist—didn't care about. He wanted freedom and equality for African Americans. The Freemasons, a respected society dedicated to liberty, equality, and peace, might help him achieve that. Boston's Freemasons had rejected him for membership, so he turned to the British Freemasons.

At British army headquarters, Sergeant John Batt led Hall and his fourteen African American friends into a private room for a solemn initiation ceremony. He taught Hall and the others the Masonic passwords, signs, and handshakes. They all swore on a Bible to keep these rituals secret and to help fellow Masons in distress. Now Prince Hall was a member of the British Freemason's Lodge of the

38th Foot Regiment, and he was ready to organize a campaign for African American civil rights.

⚬━⚬

Prince Hall may have been born in Africa or the West Indies or even in New England. The first record of him comes in 1749, when William Hall, a Boston leatherworker, or currier, bought the fourteen-year-old boy and called him Prince Hall. He soon learned the curriery trade from his master. They scoured and rubbed animal skins, doused them with grease and oil, and beat them until they were soft enough to make saddles and harnesses for horses, shoes and boots for wealthy ladies and gentlemen, and breeches and aprons for workingmen.

AFRICAN AMERICANS IN BOSTON

Hall didn't see many other black faces in Boston. Slaves might learn a trade, as Hall did, and attend a white church, but they had to sit in the African section. They could not organize their own churches or meet together in large numbers. They could not buy property or vote, but they could be sold.

Massachusetts slaves could marry, and when Hall was twenty-one he married Delia, also enslaved, and they had a son, Primus. A few years later, Delia died. Hall joined the Congregational Church, where he met and married Sarah Ritchie, who died at age twenty-four. Delia and Sarah may have died in childbirth, a common fate of many women.

In 1770, William Hall freed Prince Hall, now thirty-five, who set up his own leather-goods shop, The Golden Fleece. He married his third wife, Flora Gibbs. They had a son named Prince Africanus.

Prince Hall has lived with us 21 years and served us well upon all occasions, for which reasons we maturely give him his freedom and that he is no longer to be reckoned a slave, but has been always accounted as a freeman by us, as he has served us faithfully. Upon that account, we have given him his freedom. As witness our hands this ninth day of April, 1770.

Witnesses:
Susannah Hall   Elizabeth Hall
William Hall   Margaret Hall

SPARKS OF A REVOLUTION

Prince Hall had watched trouble brewing in Boston against British taxes. Lawyers wrote pamphlets about citizens' "natural rights" to govern themselves, workers rioted in the streets, and British army troops arrived to restore order. Some Patriots began to talk of declaring independence from Britain. They didn't include independence for slaves, though. African Americans would have to lead their own fight for freedom.

Prince Hall thought that a group like the Freemasons, or Masons, could help their cause. This was not a religion or political party but a social group dedicated to the idea of "universal brotherhood": that all people had equal worth and equal rights.

Prince Hall applied to join a Masonic Lodge in Boston, but the Masons rejected him. He suspected the reason was due to his race, because when he asked their permission to organize a separate lodge for free blacks, they refused him again. This convinced Hall that "universal brotherhood" wasn't quite universal among Boston Masons. But when he applied to the British Masons in 1775, they accepted him into their lodge.

A few weeks after Hall's initiation, the British army retreated from Boston, and the British Masonic Lodge gave Hall and his friends permission to organize their own group with a temporary charter. African Lodge No. 1, the first black Masonic Lodge in the world, elected Prince Hall as its Grand Master, or leader.

ANTISLAVERY ACTION

Hall was grateful to the British Masons. But when the Revolutionary War began, he sided with the Patriots. He wanted liberty for all Americans, black and white. There is no evidence that he fought in the war, but he did sell the Continental army five leather drumheads to help soldiers beat time on the march.

> *Boston April the 24 1777*
>
> *Col Crafts Regt of Artilery*
> *To Prince Hall for to 5 drumheads delivered*
> *at Sunday times to 9th may £1-19-0*
>
> *Rec'd above mention'd drumheads for use*
> *of Louis Reg't James Rofs—Major*
>
> *Boston 8 may 1777*
>
> *This certifys that the above drumheads*
> *are now in possession of use of the*
> *Rgt of Art'y J Sivan May Drain £1.19.0*

While soldiers fought on the battlefields, African Americans in Boston staged their own fight for freedom. On January 13, 1777, Prince Hall and seven others (four of them Masons) sent a petition to "the Honorable Counsel & House of Representatives for the State of Massachusetts Bay." They asked for an end to slavery, echoing the ideas of the Declaration of Independence.

> *The petition of A Great Number of Blackes detained in a*
> *State of Slavery in the Bowels of a free & christian Country*
> *Humbly shuwith that your Petitioners Apprehend that*
> *Thay have in Common with all other men a Natural and*
> *Unaliable Right to that freedom which the Grat Parent of the*
> *Unavese hath Bestowed equalley on all menkind.*

The Massachusetts lawmakers ignored Hall's petition.

In 1780, a new state constitution was adopted, declaring that "all men are created free and equal." Judges, not lawmakers, ended slavery in Massachusetts in 1783, declaring it unconstitutional. Soon all African Americans in Massachusetts were free. Chief Justice William Cushing of the Massachusetts Supreme Court declared

> *Our Constitution of Govmt, . . . Sets out with declaring that*
> *all men are born free & equal—& yt. Every subject is intitled*
> *to Liberty, & to have it guarded by ye. Laws, . . . & in short*
> *is totally repugnant to ye. Idea of being born Slaves. This*
> *being ye. Case I think ye. Idea of Slavery is in consistent with*
> *our own conduct & Constitution.*

BUILDING UP THE AFRICAN LODGE

After the Revolutionary War ended in 1783, Prince Hall and his African American colleagues applied to the American Masons for a permanent charter for African Lodge No. 1 but were refused. When they appealed to the British Masons in 1784, they did receive a permanent charter.

Hall wasn't the only one who recognized racism when he saw it. A white Bostonian described the situation:

> *The African Lodge, though possessing a charter from England, meet by themselves; and white masons . . . will not acknowledge them. The reason given is, that the blacks were made [Masons] clandestinely [secretly] in the first place, which, if known, would have prevented them from receiving a charter. . . . The truth is, they [white Masons] are ashamed of being on equality with blacks . . . . These [black Masons], on the other hand, . . . think themselves better masons in other respects than the whites, because masonry considers all men equal who are free, and our [Masonic] laws admit no kind of slavery.*

A Boston newspaper, reporting on a celebration by the African Lodge, sarcastically called them "St. Blacks' Lodge." Prince Hall replied with a curt letter to the editor: "Our title is not St. Black's Lodge; neither do we aspire after high titles. . . . Instead of a splendid entertainment, we had an agreeable one in brotherly love."

Prince Hall tried many ways to gain the respect of white Bostonians. As the owner of The Golden Fleece, he paid taxes and voted in local and state elections. In addition to his leather business, he ran a popular catering enterprise. One of his clients wrote:

A tall, lean Negro of great dignity, he always carried himself with the air of one who ruled many. Indeed he did, for whenever a well-to-do person wished the best catering job in eastern Massachusetts, he sent word to Prince Hall in Boston, and when the time came he appeared with a dozen of his black men, or two dozen, if the banquet was a large one.

AN END TO SLAVE TRADING

Even though Massachusetts abolished slavery in 1783, slave-trading ships continued to land in its seaports, and Prince Hall knew that African Americans were at risk. In early 1788, three men, including one African Lodge Mason, were kidnapped by a ship's captain in Boston Harbor, taken to the West Indies, and sold into slavery.

Hall and his fellow Masons, along with a group of outraged white ministers, petitioned the state government to find the men, return them to Boston, and outlaw all traces of the slave trade in Massachusetts. Hall laid out the facts of the case in their petition and then heaped flattery on the lawmakers: "knowing by Experience that your Honers have and we Trust ever Will in your Wisdom do us that Justes that our Present Condechon Requires."

In fact, Hall's petitions to the legislature were usually ignored and rarely received any justice. But this time, perhaps because white ministers joined the protest, the lawmakers listened. They passed a law preventing any slave-trading ships from entering the state, even if they were not carrying African captives. The government also sent agents to recover the three kidnapped men, who sailed back to Boston five months after their capture. Prince Hall's African Lodge threw a welcome-home party for them.

"WE . . . FEAR FOR OUR RISING OFFSPRING
TO SEE THEM IN IGNORANCE . . . AND FOR
NO OTHER REASON CAN BE GIVEN [BUT]
THIS [THAT] THEY ARE BLACK."

NO SCHOOLS FOR BLACK CHILDREN

Prince Hall knew that freedom from slavery was not the final goal for African Americans. Education was a key to progress for his people. Massachusetts provided free public schools for all white children, but Boston had no schools for black children. In 1787, Hall sent to the selectmen, or lawmakers, of Boston "a petition of a great numbers of blacks, freemen of this Commonwealth." They paid taxes and had

the right to enjoy the privileges of free men. But that we do not will appear in many instances, and we beg leave to mention one out of many, and that is of the education of our children which now receive no benefit from the free schools in the town of Boston, which we think is a great grievance, as by woful experience we now feel the want of a common education. We, therefore, must fear for our rising offspring to see them in ignorance . . . and for no other reason can be given [but] this [that] they are black.

Nothing happened. Nine years later, they were still petitioning and still being ignored.

October 4, 1796, To the gentlemen, the Selectmen, of the Town of Boston; the petition of a number of black fellow citizens of the said town.

Humbly hoping that a number of children who are destitute of the means of common education. . . . Your petitioners shall humbly hope that you gentlemen under God will take therein the childrens under your consideration and . . . that you would grant us a school house and a teacher for that end.

—Prince Hall

Finally, the Boston selectmen approved the request for a black school, but they claimed they couldn't find a single building in Boston to house it. Seeing no hope of public help, Prince Hall's son Primus opened the first black school in his home in 1798.

A DIPLOMATIC MAN

Prince Hall had become a leading spokesperson for the African American community. When a Virginia judge wrote to Jeremy Belknap, a Boston clergyman, asking about the state of affairs between blacks and whites in Massachusetts, Belknap turned to Prince Hall for an answer. Belknap knew Hall to be "a very intelligent black man," one who understood the racial climate of Boston. He asked Hall, "Does harmony in general prevail between the black and white citizens? do they associate freely together?"

Hall wrote that, legally speaking,

> *Harmony in general prevails between us as citizens, for the good law of the land does oblige every one to live peaceably with all his fellow citizens, let them be black or white. We stand on a level, therefore no pre-eminence can be claimed on either side.*

However, when it came to social acceptance, things were not "on a level."

> *As to our associating, there is here a great number of worthy good men and good citizens, that are not ashamed to take an African by the hand; but yet there are to be seen the weeds of pride, envy, tyranny, and scorn, in this garden of peace, liberty and equality.*

Prince Hall had suffered subtle prejudice and blatant discrimination. White Masonic Lodges rejected him for membership. They refused a charter for his African Lodge. State and local lawmakers ignored his many petitions and refused to provide a school for black children.

Two years after his report about the "weeds" in the "garden," Prince Hall gave a speech, later published, to his "Beloved Brethren of the African Lodge." He spoke plainly about what he and other African Americans faced every day:

> *Let us pray God that . . . he would give us the grace of patience, and strength to bear up under all our troubles, which, at this day, God knows, we have our share of. Patience, I say; for were we not possessed of a great measure of it, we could not bear up under the daily insults we meet with in the streets of Boston, much more on public days of recreation. How, at such times, are we shamefully abused, and that to such a degree, that we may truly be said to carry our lives in our hands, and the arrows of death are flying about our heads.*

Hall needed a large helping of "the grace of patience" as he worked for justice in a nonviolent, diplomatic way. As his reputation spread among African Americans, he traveled to Philadelphia to establish a second African Masonic Lodge and a third in Providence, Rhode Island.

A year after Hall's death in 1807, the African Masonic Lodges voted to change their name to "Prince Hall Lodges." Today, more than forty-five hundred Prince Hall Masonic Lodges thrive around the world with over three hundred thousand members. Though most Masonic Lodges are racially integrated now, many African Americans choose to join a Prince Hall Lodge. The legacy of Prince Hall lives on.

PART THREE

ENSLAVED WOMEN IN THE SOUTH

Southern slave owners wanted enslaved women to bear many children, because every child increased the owner's wealth. Children inherited their mother's status, so enslaved women bore enslaved children, even if those children had free fathers and even if the father was the owner himself.

New mothers weren't coddled. They received a new blanket and a short break from work after they gave birth. A few days or weeks later, enslaved mothers returned to work and left their babies with a woman who was too old to take on any other job.

Family life for slaves was fragile. Owners or ministers might "marry" couples, but this had no legal standing. Owners could break up marriages by selling husband or wife. If slaves chose marriage partners from different plantations, they had to live apart. Wives and children could see their husbands and fathers only on Sundays, their one day off.

Women often had full charge of raising their children and making a home. And every mother knew she could be ripped away from her children at the whim of her owner.

YEARNING FOR FREEDOM

Women as well as men yearned for freedom, but running away was an unlikely option for mothers. A woman with children in tow wouldn't stand much chance of outrunning slave patrols and tracking dogs. During the Revolutionary War era, fewer than 10 percent of the runaway-slave notices in Virginia newspapers mentioned women.

Mary Perth, Ona Judge, and Sally Hemings all felt the push toward freedom and the pull of home and family. When Mary Perth learned that the British offered her freedom, she dared to leave home with her three young children and escape to a British army camp. Throughout her long life, she had to leave many homes behind and create new ones in New York, Canada, and Africa.

Ona Judge, owned by Martha Washington, grew up at Mount Vernon. At age fifteen, she was taken north when George Washington became president. Ona had a choice: continuing a fairly comfortable life with the Washingtons or escaping to the unknown world of freedom. If she chose freedom, she would never see her family again.

Sally Hemings lived among her mother, aunts, uncles, brothers, and sisters—all owned by Thomas Jefferson. As a teenager, she was sent to Paris, France, to serve the daughters of Jefferson, who was stationed there as the U.S. minister. Hemings could have stayed in France as a free woman because French law didn't allow slavery. But home and family pulled her back to Virginia, though not before she made a risky bargain with Jefferson.

Three southern women, tied to home and family, heard the cry for freedom, considered their choices, and traveled different roads toward that goal.

CHAPTER SEVEN

MARY PERTH

(ca. 1740–1813)

On a fine day in late September 1794, a ship flying the British flag sailed into the harbor of Freetown, a British colony in Sierra Leone, West Africa. A crowd of people gathered to greet the ship when suddenly the crew opened fire. A seven-year-old boy was killed outright, one woman had her leg blown off, and people ran for their lives.

The ship was not British but French, and France was at war with Britain. The governor of Freetown raised a white flag of truce, but the shooting continued for an hour and a half. Then French sailors invaded the town to loot or destroy everything in sight.

Amid the chaos, Mary Perth kept her head. She ran to the governor's school to save the twenty-five African boys who lived and studied there. They joined the stream of terrified settlers racing inland toward safety in the woods and mountains. Back in Freetown, Mary's house, her shop, and all the goods she had to sell lay open to looters. But she chose to save the children.

Mary and the boys took refuge in a nearby village, and Pa Demba, the village headman, gave them food and shelter for the next two weeks. Meanwhile, the French burned every official building in Freetown along with ten settlers' homes and eight boats. They ransacked the town library, wrecked a new printing press, and killed twelve hundred hogs and all the poultry.

When the French finally left, Mary returned with the boys. All the goods in her shop had been stolen, but she *had* saved the children.

Mary's early years are lost to history. No one knows if she was born in Africa or America or who her parents were. She first appeared in a 1767 tax record that reported that young Mary had been bought by John Willoughby, a rich planter in Norfolk County, Virginia. Mary, about twenty-eight years old, with three young children, was put to work cooking, scrubbing floors, and perhaps caring for the Willoughby children.

MIDNIGHT PREACHER

Mary learned to read somehow, though few slaves did. She also became a Christian and a preacher. Slave gatherings, including religious meetings, were forbidden in Virginia. So late at night when her owners, the Willoughbys, were asleep, Mary tied her baby to her back and walked ten miles out of Norfolk and into the Great Dismal Swamp to lead secret prayer meetings.

Mary preached sermons, and the group sang hymns about the promise of heaven to all good Christians, regardless of their color. When the meeting was over, Mary walked back to Norfolk, arriving before the family awoke, to work another day.

Most white people in Virginia were Anglican, the official Church of England, where services were formal and included complicated sermons. Mary was a Methodist. Methodists' sermons appealed to people's emotions. Worshipers were encouraged to testify—tell personal stories—about their spiritual lives, and the services were filled with singing and shouting.

The Anglicans were horrified by such behavior. To make matters worse, many Methodist preachers opposed slavery, and owners didn't want their slaves hearing that message. The mayor of Norfolk ran one white Methodist preacher out of town, saying, "If we permit such a fellow as this to come here we shall have an insurrection of the Negroes."

So Mary and her friends met in the woods at night.

PATRIOTS AND LOYALISTS

Other issues worried Virginia slave owners. By 1775, fighting had begun in Massachusetts, and Americans were choosing sides. Mary's owner, John Willoughby, a royal lieutenant, was arrested as a Loyalist by the Patriots. Willoughby denied the charge, claimed he was a true Patriot, and was released. But the Patriots didn't trust him and ordered him to move thirty miles inland, away from the royal governor, Lord Dunmore. The Patriots also ordered Willoughby's slaves seized.

All of Willoughby's slaves, fearing that they would be sold by the Patriots, escaped to Dunmore, who had promised to free them. Eighty-seven men, women, and children, including Mary and her three young daughters, became free Black Loyalists.

But disaster struck: a smallpox epidemic killed hundreds of people who took refuge with Dunmore. Then typhoid killed hundreds more. Only six of Willoughby's eighty-seven former slaves survived, among them Mary and her daughters.

In July 1776, she and her girls climbed aboard a British ship bound for New York City. They lived out the war there, along with thousands of other former slaves. In British-held New York, she was free. No one asked her for a written pass to prove she had permission to walk freely down the street. No one forced her to work without wages. No one owned her or her children.

WARTIME NEW YORK CITY

Mary's life in wartime New York was not easy. Tents, shacks, and houses sprang up in "Canvas Town" to shelter the Black Loyalists. Women like Mary worked as cooks, laundresses, and seamstresses. Black Loyalist men labored as carpenters to rebuild the city that had been burned by retreating Patriots. Black Loyalist musicians entertained at balls and taverns, and others worked as servants of British officers.

> **"ALL NEGROES THAT FLY FROM THE ENEMY'S COUNTRY ARE FREE—NO PERSON WHATEVER CAN CLAIM A RIGHT TO THEM."**

In 1779, the British repeated their promise of freedom: "All Negroes that fly from the enemy's country are free—No person whatever can claim a right to them—Whoever sells them shall be prosecuted with the utmost severity." Hundreds more people thronged to freedom in New York, including Caesar Perth, a carpenter.

Both he and Mary came from Norfolk. Perhaps they knew each other there; perhaps Caesar was the father of Mary's daughters. Enslaved couples in the south were not allowed to marry, but free people in New York could, and young Mary became Mary Perth. "Daddy" Moses Wilkinson, a popular Methodist preacher, probably married them. Though blind and crippled from smallpox, he attracted a large congregation.

A DANGEROUS PEACE

When the Americans won the war, Mary and her family found themselves in danger. The peace treaty demanded that the British should not "[carry] away any negroes or other property of the American inhabitants." Americans wanted their slaves back. John Willoughby had died, but his son came to New York to recapture the family "property."

However, British commander in chief Sir Guy Carleton refused General George Washington's demand to surrender the Black Loyalists because they were no longer "property" but free men and women. He declared that never would the British government "reduce themselves to the necessity of violating their faith to the Negroes. Delivering up Negroes to their former masters . . . would be a dishonourable violation of the public faith."

> **"DELIVERING UP NEGROES TO THEIR FORMER MASTERS . . . WOULD BE A DISHONOURABLE VIOLATION OF THE PUBLIC FAITH."**

When Washington repeated his demand for the return of the slaves, Carleton spelled it out even more clearly: "The Negroes in question, I have already said, I found free when I arrived at New York, I had therefore no right, as I thought, to prevent their going to any part of the world they thought proper."

NO PROMISED LAND

Mary and Caesar Perth thought it "proper" to sail to Nova Scotia on the eastern shore of Canada with Moses Wilkinson and his Methodists.

The Book of Negroes that listed the passengers described Mary, forty-three, as a "stout wench," which means "strong woman."

The Perth family helped to build Birchtown, a black community near the town of Shelburne, and their daughter, Susan, was born there. The Black Loyalists had brought their religion to Nova Scotia. One visiting white minister counted fourteen different Methodist groups that met every night. Another complained about their "pious frenzy." They were still singing, shouting, and testifying with enthusiasm. Mary may have led some of the prayer meetings and taught reading and writing to children and adults.

But Nova Scotia was not Mary and Caesar Perth's promised land. The Black Loyalists had their freedom, but they did not have the right to vote or to serve on juries. Black workers earned meager wages and some earned no wages at all, working like slaves for just food and lodging. White men held all the power in the province.

ANOTHER CHANCE

When John Clarkson, a white Englishman, spoke one night at Moses Wilkinson's church, Mary, Caesar, and hundreds more crowded in to hear him. Clarkson and a group of abolitionists in England had formed the private Sierra Leone Company to settle Black Loyalists on the west coast of Africa.

For centuries, African tribesmen had been selling their enemy captives to white slave traders. Clarkson described how Black Loyalists would prosper by farming and trading with Africans and Europeans. They could show the Africans a more ethical way to make a living. The Sierra Leone Company promised the Black Loyalists land and self-government.

Clarkson had hoped to recruit one hundred settlers for the colony. Instead, he enlisted twelve hundred, including Moses Wilkinson's entire Methodist congregation. First on Clarkson's list of settlers were Mary, Susan, and Caesar Perth, along with Mary's three grown daughters and their families. Surely Sierra Leone would be their promised land.

A NEW LIFE IN AFRICA

In March 1792, after a stormy voyage across the Atlantic, the ships neared the coast of Sierra Leone. Warm breezes blew them into the harbor. As they left the ship and stepped onto the shore of Africa, they sang a favorite hymn:

> *Awake! and sing the song*
> *of Moses and the Lamb,*
> *Wake! every heart and every tongue*
> *To praise the Saviour's name! . . .*
> *The day of Jubilee is come;*
> *Return ye ransomed sinners home.*

Mary cared for her young daughter Susan, while Caesar worked with the men to clear the jungle and build Freetown. The first houses were African-style huts—woven branches plastered with mud and covered by a thatched grass roof. When the three-month-long monsoon rains began in April, the storms tore off the roofs and brought out the biting, stinging insects that invaded homes and food supplies. Malaria and other fevers and intestinal illnesses killed so many that the settlers couldn't hold proper burials until the rainy season ended.

But Mary and her fellow Nova Scotians were determined to make this colony work. She and Caesar received seven acres of land from the Sierra Leone Company, and Caesar built a two-story wooden house to withstand the fierce rains. The settlers built a school for Susan and the other children. The Black Loyalists had not taken on this dangerous adventure just for themselves. They wrote: "We have feeling the same as other Human Beings and would wish . . . to make our Children free and happy."

> **"WE HAVE FEELING THE SAME AS OTHER HUMAN BEINGS AND WOULD WISH . . . TO MAKE OUR CHILDREN FREE AND HAPPY."**

ON HER OWN

Just a few months after they arrived in Africa, Caesar Perth died, probably of a tropical disease. Mary, fifty-two years old, now had to support herself and her young daughter. She sold her farmland and took in paying lodgers. She was one of the first settlers to receive a license to open a shop in Freetown, and as the head of a household, she could vote for members of the local community coucil—a radical notion.

> **"THERE IS ONE OLD WOMAN . . . (NAMED MARY PERTH). . . . SHE IS MORE LIKE ONE COME DOWN OUT OF HEAVEN TO EARTH, THAN LIKE ONE WHO IS ONLY PREPARING FOR GLORY."**
>
> —*Rev. Mr. Clark*

The English governor, Zachary Macaulay, hired Mary Perth, "the good old woman," as his housekeeper as well as housemother and tutor for his school for African boys.

When Macaulay brought an Anglican minister to Freetown, Mary proved to be a master of diplomacy. The Reverend Mr. Clark hoped to draw people away from the "enthusiastic" Methodists to the more "respectable" Anglicans. Clark exhorted the Methodists to come to the Anglican Christ. They responded, "We don't want you . . . we are in Christ already and have been for these last 22 years." But Mary attended Clark's church, the only Methodist to do so, and he praised her in an English church magazine:

> *She is the best assistant I have here, next to my Bible. . . .*
> *It is so pleasant to hear her talk with a child-like simplic-*
> *ity, yet with a celestial sublimity, about divine things. . . .*
> *I need not tell you she is a black. This I can assure you is*
> *no hindrance to our Christian fellowship. I am as happy*
> *in her company, and in that of some others, as ever I was*
> *in that of any Christian of my own colour.*

Despite Clark's patronizing tone, he respected Mary Perth. Though she went to his Anglican church, she didn't desert the Methodists. She also attended Moses Wilkinson's services with her old friends. She seemed to get along with everyone—for a while.

QUARRELS WITH THE GOVERNOR

Over time, Governor Macaulay turned against his housekeeper, declaring Mary had become "vain, worldly, and arrogant, harsh and violent in her tempers." He complained about her "most unchristian . . . rage, revenge, impatience, and pride." Apparently, the two had quarreled, and Mary wasn't afraid to express her "rage" and "impatience." When Mary apologized for her part in the quarrel, Macaulay didn't accept it, calling it "the common Methodist cant."

He claimed that her successful businesses seemed to "unhinge her mind, to fill her with pride and with all those bad tempers." He accused her of being "little attentive to discharge the duties to the children under her care." So he fired her.

Other English visitors also found the Freetown settlers too proud. One white woman, interviewing a black woman to be a servant, reported, "She seemed not to consider herself at all inferior, for she walked across the room and took possession of the sofa with the greatest composure in the world, and insisted on shaking hands with me."

FORGIVEN

Some months after Governor Macaulay's outburst against Mary, he forgave her many "faults." Perhaps he couldn't run his school without her. He planned to take his African boys to England to train as

Christian missionaries, and he wanted Mary to come with him. She would be in charge of them once more.

Mary was eager to go, because her daughter Susan, fifteen years old, was ailing, and England offered better medical treatment than Freetown did. Sadly, Susan died in England. After two years, in 1801, Mary returned to Freetown and her thriving businesses and, at age sixty-six, she married again.

When she died in 1813, it's likely that Moses Wilkinson preached a rousing funeral sermon for Mary Perth. Her spirit never faltered as she escaped from slavery in wartime America, to freedom in the Nova Scotia wilderness, and finally to a modest prosperity in Sierra Leone.

CHAPTER EIGHT

ONA JUDGE

(1773–1848)

It was an ordinary day for Martha Washington, the president's wife, but not for her enslaved maid, Ona Judge. In the morning, Ona laid out Martha's clothes and combed Martha's hair—as usual. Mrs. Washington received friends and official guests—as usual. In the early afternoon, the Washingtons sat down to dinner—as usual. Ona ate in the kitchen with the other slaves—as usual. But on that day, she didn't wait for Mrs. Washington to send for her. Instead, she walked out the back door of the president's house onto the streets of Philadelphia.

She saw crowds of people going about their business. Some were free African Americans, many of them ragged and poor, forced to work for low wages, if they found work at all. Ona was well fed, well dressed, and well liked by Mrs. Washington. Yet Ona was walking away from her mistress. She knocked at the door of a friend's house, then slipped inside. Her flight to freedom had begun.

Ona Judge grew up at Mount Vernon, George Washington's Virginia plantation. Her father, Andrew Judge, a white Englishman, had been an indentured servant, bound to work at Mount Vernon for four years. He left in 1776 when he fulfilled his contract and Ona never saw her father again. Her mother, Betty, a skilled spinner, weaver, and seamstress, was a "dower slave," part of the wealth that Martha Washington, a young widow, brought with her when she married George. Because Betty was enslaved, so was Ona.

> **"SHE HAS BEEN THE PARTICULAR ATTENDANT ON MRS. WASHINGTON SINCE SHE WAS TEN YEARS OLD; AND WAS HANDY AND USEFUL TO HER BEING PERFECT MISTRESS OF HER NEEDLE."**
>
> —*George Washington*

Young Ona Judge learned fine sewing skills from her mother. Together they knitted stockings, embroidered baby gowns, and sewed shirts for men and fine dresses for women. Martha Washington, who sometimes joined their sewing circle, praised Ona as a "perfect Mistress of her needle."

When George Washington was elected president of the new United States in 1789, Martha took a few of her favorite slaves north to New York and then Philadelphia, the temporary capitals. Ona Judge and her half brother, Austin, were among them. Austin waited on the table in the presidential dining room. Fifteen-year-old Ona became Martha's personal maid.

LIFE IN PHILADELPHIA

Ona walked freely through Philadelphia as she ran errands for her mistress. She saw ships arriving from overseas, sailors speaking foreign languages, peddlers shouting their wares, and shops of all kinds. The Washingtons gave her money to go to the circus, theatrical plays, and a show of acrobats. How different from her quiet rural life at Mount Vernon.

Ona made friends in the growing community of free black men and women who were forming social clubs and churches. They told her about abolitionists, both black and white, who lobbied lawmakers to abolish slavery.

For several years, rumors circulated among Washington's slaves that George and Martha might free them when the couple died. Ona Judge was in her early twenties by then, and the Washingtons were in their sixties, an advanced age in that era. If the rumors were true, Ona might gain her freedom while she was still a young woman. So it was a shock when Martha told Ona one day that when Martha died she planned to give Ona to her granddaughter.

> **"I HAD FRIENDS AMONG THE COLORED PEOPLE OF PHILADELPHIA."**
>
> —*Ona Judge*

Escaping to freedom wouldn't be easy. As Martha Washington's slave, Ona was well known and would have a hard time hiding. If she were caught, she would probably be punished and might be sold. If she did escape, she could never return to Virginia to see her family. She would have to live among strangers and earn her own living. But her free friends had advantages that she wanted. Some could read and write. They went to their own churches on Sunday. They were free to choose their course in life.

When she was twenty-two, Ona Judge made her choice. Every summer, the Washingtons returned to Mount Vernon with Ona. In May 1796, "Whilst they were packing up to go to Virginia, I was packing to go, I didn't know where; for I knew that if I went back to Virginia, I should never get my liberty," she said.

GONE BUT NOT SAFE

On May 21, Ona Judge pretended to leave the house on Mrs. Washington's business. But instead, she hid with African American friends. She knew Washington would search for her, and she was right. Three days later, notices appeared in two Philadelphia newspapers:

> ABSCONDED *from the household of the President of the United States,* ONEY JUDGE, *a slight mulatto girl, much freckled, with very black eyes and bushy black hair. She is of middle stature, slender, and delicately formed; about 20 years of age. She has many changes of good clothes, of all sorts.*

Ona's escape took everyone by surprise. The ad continued, "There was no suspicion of her going off nor no provocation to do so."

> *But as she may attempt an escape by water, all masters of vessels are cautioned against admitting her into them, although it is probable she will attempt to pass for a free woman, and has, it is said, wherewithal [money] to pay her passage.*

A ten-dollar reward was offered "to any person" for her return, and even more if she were caught far from Philadelphia.

The best reason the Washingtons could conjure up to explain Ona's escape was a romantic adventure. They invented a Frenchman who must have lured her away, for how could such a young uneducated woman escape alone?

Ona did it with help from her African American friends—and a big dose of courage. They found a ship sailing to Portsmouth, New Hampshire, under Captain John Bowles. But Ona wasn't safe yet. She still had to walk through the streets full of people, who would

ON MAY 10, 1796, WASHINGTON'S HOUSEHOLD ACCOUNT BOOK REPORTS THAT ONA JUDGE, "MRS. WASHINGTON'S GIRL," WAS GIVEN $1.25 TO BUY NEW SHOES. ON MAY 21, SHE "ABSCONDED," PROBABLY WEARING HER NEW SHOES.

want that ten-dollar reward, to the wharf where "all masters of vessels" were warned of her. Helping any slave escape was illegal, and defying the president of the United States was sure to bring trouble.

Perhaps Captain Bowles took the risk because he was a New England man, and by 1796 New Englanders had turned against slavery. Ona later said, "I never told his name till after he died, . . . lest they should punish him for bringing me away."

Washington wrote to a friend in New York, asking him to search for Ona. The friend found "a free mulattoe [mixed-race] Woman" who

"I NEVER TOLD HIS NAME TILL AFTER HE DIED, . . . LEST THEY SHOULD PUNISH HIM FOR BRINGING ME AWAY."

knew Ona and declared that she had come to New York but then left for Boston. Washington's friend wasn't sure he believed the woman's story. "Whether this last information is intended as a blind [bluff] or not I cannot say, however I have spoken to a Constable [policeman] of the City who has promised me to keep a watch & make search for her." The woman's story was a bluff—Ona had sailed to New Hampshire, not Boston—but it shows that the African American network was a wide one that protected its own.

Washington's web of influence was even wider.

WASHINGTON'S WIDE WEB

After arriving safely in Portsmouth, New Hampshire, Ona Judge made friends with the few African Americans in town and took work as a seamstress and house servant. Then one day on the street, a young white woman called her name. Elizabeth Langdon, daughter of U.S. senator John Langdon, lived in Portsmouth and had met Ona in Philadelphia. When Elizabeth asked her what she was doing in Portsmouth, she fled. Washington was sure to learn of her whereabouts now.

> **"TO SEIZE, AND PUT HER ON BOARD A VESSEL . . . SEEMS AT FIRST VIEW, TO BE THE SAFEST AND LEAST EXPENSIVE [PLAN]."**

He did, and he set about getting her back.

Congress had passed a Fugitive Slave Law to recover runaway slaves. When a slave owner appeared before a judge and proved his ownership, the captured runaway was handed over to him. But people in New Hampshire opposed slavery. If the president were to reenslave Ona Judge, it would have caused an uproar.

So Washington sent orders to Portsmouth: "To seize, and put her on board a Vessel . . . seems at first view, to be the safest and least expensive [plan]." It was probably Martha's idea. She was angry and hurt; her favorite maid had turned disloyal and run away.

Joseph Whipple, a federal employee in Portsmouth, took on the task. The day before a ship was due to sail for Virginia, he asked Ona to visit him, saying that his family wanted to hire a servant. When she arrived, Whipple announced that she had to return to the Washingtons.

Ona bravely replied that she respected her master and mistress and missed her family in Virginia. She would return to Mount Vernon if the Washingtons promised to free her when they died. But she would rather die than be sold to anyone else, for she had "a thirst for compleat freedom." Whipple promised that he would make sure that the Washingtons eventually freed her, and Ona agreed to board the ship the next day.

> **"SHE SHOULD RATHER SUFFER DEATH THAN RETURN TO SLAVERY & LIABLE TO BE SOLD OR GIVEN TO ANY OTHER PERSON."**
>
> —Joseph Whipple

STILL IN DANGER

That evening, Ona's friends warned her that even if Whipple tried to secure her freedom, there was no guarantee he would succeed. She took their advice, and the ship sailed without her. Whipple wrote to the president, explaining what had happened.

Washington was furious that Whipple had let her slip away. He refused to consider her request to be freed when Martha died. Such a promise would encourage more slaves to escape, then bargain for their freedom. Try again, Washington wrote. Seize her and send her back, but do it quietly. If the action became public, it might incite a riot. If Whipple couldn't kidnap her in secret, leave Ona alone, the president ordered.

Whipple tried again to convince Ona to return to the Washingtons. She refused and revealed that she was engaged to a free black sailor.

This doomed Whipple's plan. Local people would certainly object to seizing the wife of a freeman. But Whipple wanted to please the president, so he ordered the town clerk to delay the marriage. Instead, Ona and Jack Staines, her fiancé, went to a neighboring town to get married.

A year later, Ona gave birth to a daughter and her husband went off to sea again. While he was gone, Martha Washington's nephew, Burwell Bassett, Jr., came to visit Senator Langdon in Portsmouth. George Washington asked Bassett to try one more time to bring Ona back peacefully—no kidnapping, no violence.

WASHINGTON'S LAST TRY

Bassett knocked on Ona's door when she was home alone with her baby. He told her that if she returned to his aunt Martha, she would be forgiven and freed. This was a lie and Ona knew it. She replied, "I am free now and choose to remain so." Later that day, dining with the

Langdons, Bassett announced that he planned to kidnap Ona and her child.

"I AM FREE NOW AND CHOOSE TO REMAIN SO."

Senator Langdon was a friend of Washington's, but he was a New England man first. He sent a message to Ona, told her Bassett's plan, and advised her to leave town. She hired a wagon, took her baby, and traveled to a nearby town where she hid with a free black family. When news came that Bassett had left Portsmouth, she returned home.

Ona later said, "They never troubled me any more after [Bassett] was gone." But she didn't know that at the time. In his will, George Washington eventually freed all his slaves. But Ona belonged to Martha, and she didn't free her slaves. Philadelphia Judge, Ona's sister and also a dower slave, was freed in 1807 by Martha's granddaughter, who had inherited her when Martha died. If Ona had not escaped, maybe she, too, would have been freed. Or maybe not.

NO REGRETS

Ona Judge Staines lived out her long life as a free woman. She chose a husband and married him legally, something an enslaved Virginian could not do. She bore three children, Eliza, Nancy, and William. Because their mother was enslaved, they were legally enslaved as well. But they lived free in New Hampshire.

Jack Staines died at sea in 1803, when Ona was just thirty, leaving her to raise her three small children. She worked as a house servant, sharing a home with a free African American family, a father and two sisters. Her son, William, became a sailor like his father and was lost at sea. Eliza and Nancy both died before their mother passed away. That left Judge and the two sisters to live out their days in Greenland,

New Hampshire. In their last years, they depended on the charity of their neighbors.

In 1846, when she was seventy-three, Ona Judge gave two newspaper interviews. She was old and poor and admitted that she had suffered hardship and even danger. But she chose freedom and never regretted it.

She fulfilled her dream of learning to read and write, and she became a devout Christian. None of these advantages were offered to her at Mount Vernon. As for her hard times, surely Ona felt they were a fair price to pay for freedom.

"I AM FREE, AND HAVE, I TRUST BEEN MADE A CHILD OF GOD."

—Ona Judge

CHAPTER NINE

SALLY HEMINGS

(1773–1835)

Sally Hemings, sixteen years old and pregnant, faced the hardest choice of her life: freedom in a foreign land or slavery at home in Virginia.

Two years earlier, she had moved from a slave's cabin to a mansion in Paris to serve her owner, Thomas Jefferson, the first U.S. minister (ambassador) to France. Now, in 1789, Thomas Jefferson was returning to Virginia. Sally could go home to her mother, her brothers and sisters, aunts, uncles, and cousins, but she and her child would be enslaved.

Slavery was illegal in France. If she stayed, she and her child could be free. But she would have to make her way alone in a foreign country: find a home, a job to support herself and her child, and a community of friends. Besides that, violent mobs had begun to riot in the Paris streets, rebelling against wretched poverty and inequality that dogged their lives. Royal troops prowled the city and attacked the mobs. The bloody French Revolution had begun.

Sally could choose a dangerous freedom or familiar slavery . . . or perhaps she could strike a bargain with Thomas Jefferson, the father of her unborn child.

Sally was Elizabeth (Betty) Hemings's sixth child fathered by her owner, John Wayles. He died when Sally was a baby, and his daughter, Martha, Thomas Jefferson's wife, inherited the Hemings family. So Sally grew up at Monticello, the Jefferson family home, alongside her half sister, Martha.

Betty Hemings and her sons worked as personal servants to Jefferson, rather than as field hands. Light-skinned slaves, or "bright mulattoes," were often preferred as house slaves. But there was a more likely reason for their special treatment: they were related to Martha Jefferson. Sally began working when she was eight years old, as a maid for Patsy, Jefferson's older daughter.

> **"BETTY WAS A BRIGHT [LIGHT-SKINNED] MULATTO WOMAN, AND SALLY MIGHTY NEAR WHITE. . . . FOLKS SAID THAT THESE HEMINGSES WAS OLD MR. WAYLES' CHILDREN."**
>
> —*Isaac Jefferson, Monticello slave*

INVADED

In 1781, the British army invaded Virginia and tried to kidnap Thomas Jefferson, the governor at the time, in Richmond, the capital. He and his family fled to Monticello, about seventy miles away, but the British troops followed him there, and they fled again.

Sally's family and the other slaves were left defenseless at Monticello. For a day and a night, the enemy soldiers swarmed the house and grounds looking for Jefferson and valuables to steal. Sally huddled with her family in the slave quarters, but the troops left without harming them.

A LONG WAY FROM HOME

After the war, Jefferson, a widower now, moved to Paris as the first U.S. minister. His daughter Patsy, eleven, went with him, and Polly, six, stayed in Virginia with relatives. Sally Hemings, just eleven, had to leave her family at Monticello to serve as Polly's maid.

Three years later, in 1787, Jefferson, desperately missing Polly, arranged for her and an older woman to come to Paris. That woman had just given birth, so Sally Hemings was sent instead. She traveled with eight-year-old Polly across the Atlantic to London, where Abigail and John Adams, the U.S. minister to Great Britain, met them.

Abigail wrote to Jefferson that she found Sally "good naturd" but "quite a child." And so she was, just four-teen years old, not only far from home among strangers but with a child in her care. "Good-natured" Sally possessed both courage and emotional maturity.

When Sally reached Paris, the most welcome sight was her brother James, who was studying gourmet cooking with a French chef in Jefferson's kitchen. James could help her find her way in a strange country where people spoke another language.

> # "SALLY WAS VERY HANDSOME: LONG STRAIGHT HAIR DOWN HER BACK."
>
> —*Israel Jefferson, Monticello slave*

Polly joined her sister, Patsy, at a French Catholic boarding school, and Sally looked after both of them each weekend, when they returned to their father.

Sally accompanied Patsy to dinners, concerts, plays, and balls, wearing elegant French fashions, though not quite as elegant as Patsy's. During the week, she had time to explore the streets of Paris and begin to learn French.

With little work to do for the two girls, Sally became Thomas Jefferson's personal servant. As her French improved, she met free black men and women, immigrants from Africa and former slaves from the French Caribbean islands. She learned that slavery was illegal in France and that as long as she lived there, she was free. Jefferson knew this, too, and paid Sally for her work, something unknown to his slaves back in Virginia.

A GREAT DECISION

During her two years in Paris, Sally Hemings, a teenager, and forty-six-year-old Thomas Jefferson began a sexual relationship. A fellow slave described Sally as "mighty near white" and "very handsome [with] long straight hair down her back." She was called "Dashing Sally" and may have even resembled her half sister, Martha, Jefferson's wife.

> **"SALLY HEMINGS . . . WAS EMPLOYED AS HIS CHAMBER-MAID, AND THAT MR. JEFFERSON WAS ON THE MOST INTIMATE TERMS WITH HER; . . . IN FACT, SHE WAS HIS CONCUBINE."**
>
> —Israel Jefferson

As Jefferson planned his return to Virginia, Sally learned she was pregnant. She knew that if she stayed in France, she must wend her way through a maze of bureaucracy—in a foreign language, in a country in revolt—to appear before a French judge and request a certificate of freedom. Only then would she and her child be free. Back in Virginia, home and family awaited her, but she would be enslaved again.

At first, Sally refused to return. She would stay in France as a free woman. Then Jefferson turned on his powers of persuasion. After all, he had written the Declaration of Independence, which helped persuade thirteen colonies to revolt against the British Empire!

According to Madison Hemings, their son, Jefferson "promised [Sally] extraordinary privileges, and made a solemn pledge that her children should be freed at the age of twenty-one years." So Sally Hemings returned home to become a privileged slave. Her children would receive a greater privilege—freedom.

Sally Hemings took a risk trusting Jefferson. He put nothing in writing. He could have changed his mind at any time, and Sally would have had no way to hold him to his promise. But sixteen-year-old Sally weighed her options and took a chance on Jefferson.

LIFE AT MONTICELLO

Back at Monticello in 1789, Sally took up her light household work, sewing, and errands. Sally's first child "lived but a short time," and Jefferson didn't record the birth in his Farm Book accounts. Over the next nineteen years, Sally gave birth to six children with Jefferson, the last born when she was thirty-five and Jefferson, sixty-five. Two daughters died in infancy, but three sons (Beverly, Madison, and Eston) and one daughter (Harriet) lived to adulthood.

Sally remained at Monticello when Jefferson left home to become secretary of state, then vice president and president. He returned now and then for visits and finally retired to Monticello in 1809, when he was sixty-six.

HER CHILDREN GROW UP

During these years, Sally lived in the shadow of Jefferson's promise. Her special treatment caused jealousy among the other slaves, and her intimate relationship with Jefferson was common knowledge.

One slave reported, "When Madison Hemings declares that he is a natural son of Thomas Jefferson . . . and that his brothers Beverly and Eston and sister Harriet are of the same parentage, I can as conscientiously confirm his statement as any other fact which I believe from circumstances but do not positively know."

Rumors of Sally and her children traveled beyond Monticello. Jefferson's political opponents published insulting stories about "Dusky Sally," but Jefferson refused to answer any of these attacks in public speeches or private letters. However, the evidence was plain to see.

One "gentleman dining with Mr. Jefferson, looked so startled as he raised his eyes from the latter to the servant [a Hemings son] behind him, that his discovery of the resemblance was perfectly obvious to all. . . . The likeness between master and slave was blazoned to all the multitudes who visited."

Sally Hemings lived quietly at Monticello as her children grew up. Madison recalled, "It was her duty, all her life which I can remember, up to the time of father's death, to take care of his chamber and wardrobe, look after us children and do such light work as sewing."

> "WE WERE FREE FROM THE DREAD OF HAVING TO BE SLAVES ALL OUR LIVES LONG, AND WERE MEASURABLY HAPPY."

FATHER AND SONS

Jefferson never acknowledged Sally's children as his own, but she told them that Jefferson was their father and that he would free them when they grew up. Jefferson "was uniformly kind to all about him," but showed no "fatherly affection to us children," said Madison. Still, "we were free from the dread of having to be slaves all our lives long, and were measurably happy. We were always permitted to be with our mother."

Jefferson, an accomplished violinist with a fine tenor voice, passed on his musical talents to his Hemings sons. Sally listened as all three boys learned to play the violin, and Beverly performed for the Jeffersons at their family parties. Eston later became a professional musician.

Sally saw Jefferson apprentice their children to skilled trades that would serve them well when they were free. Daughter Harriet learned to spin and weave. Sons Beverly, Madison, and Eston became carpenters and cabinetmakers, taught by their uncle John Hemings.

The three young men worked with John to build a smaller version of Monticello at Poplar Forest, ninety miles from Monticello. Jefferson, who loved building and rebuilding his homes, spent weeks and months alongside his Hemings sons at Poplar Forest. Far away from the prying eyes of Jefferson's white family and jealous slaves, perhaps father and sons developed a closer relationship.

A PLEDGE FULFILLED

In 1822, Sally saw Jefferson's "solemn pledge" honored for the first time. When Beverly, twenty-three, left Monticello, no notices for a runaway slave were issued and no manhunt took place. His siblings knew where he had gone, and perhaps Jefferson knew as well. A few months later, Sally said good-bye to Harriet.

Jefferson's white overseer reported:

> *Jefferson . . . freed one girl some years before he died, and there was a great deal of talk about it. She was nearly as white as anybody, and very beautiful. People said he freed her because she was his own daughter. . . . By Mr. Jefferson's direction I paid her stage fare to Philadelphia, and gave her fifty dollars.*

Jefferson noted in his inventory of slaves: "Beverly run away 22 [1822]" and "Harriet. Sally's [daughter] run [away] 22 [1822.]."

According to their brother Madison, Beverly and Harriet "passed" into the white world of Washington, D.C., and never returned to Monticello. They both changed their names, married into white families, and raised children who never knew their parents' history. Though Madison kept in touch with them, he never publicly revealed their new identities.

LIFE AFTER JEFFERSON

Sally Hemings's younger sons, Madison and Eston, didn't leave Monticello when they were twenty-one. They stayed with their mother. When Jefferson died in 1826, he freed only five of his 130 slaves—all of them from the Hemings family, including Eston and Madison.

He didn't free Sally, who was fifty-three. Instead, Patsy, probably obeying her father's wish, gave Sally "her time," which was an unofficial freedom sometimes granted to older slaves. Sally, Eston, and Madison moved to nearby Charlottesville and lived together until Sally's death at age sixty-two, in 1835.

After Sally died, the two brothers moved to Ohio, married, and raised large families. Eston Hemings went on to Wisconsin, changed his name to Eston Jefferson, passed into white society, and earned his living as a musician. Madison Hemings stayed in Ohio, working as a carpenter and a

> "HIS DEATH WAS AN AFFAIR OF GREAT MOMENT AND UNCERTAINTY TO US SLAVES, FOR MR. JEFFERSON PROVIDED FOR THE FREEDOM OF [5] SERVANTS ONLY."
>
> —Israel Jefferson

farmer. In 1873, he gave an interview about his family background that was published in Ohio's *Pike County Republican.*

Sally Hemings left no letters or diaries, and many questions remain unanswered: Did she regret the decision she made as a teenager in Paris? Did she long for freedom from her "gilded cage" of slavery? How did she feel about Jefferson never acknowledging their children as his own? Did she mourn when her two older children passed out of her life and into white society?

Although she had very little negotiating power as a slave, Sally used her position to her advantage and lived a comfortable life surrounded by her family. She was the only woman at Monticello who saw all her children freed.

Sally Hemings and Thomas Jefferson apparently remained faithful to each other for thirty-seven years. They shared a family, and Jefferson fulfilled his "solemn pledge." As for Sally Hemings, she staged a risky campaign for freedom—and won.

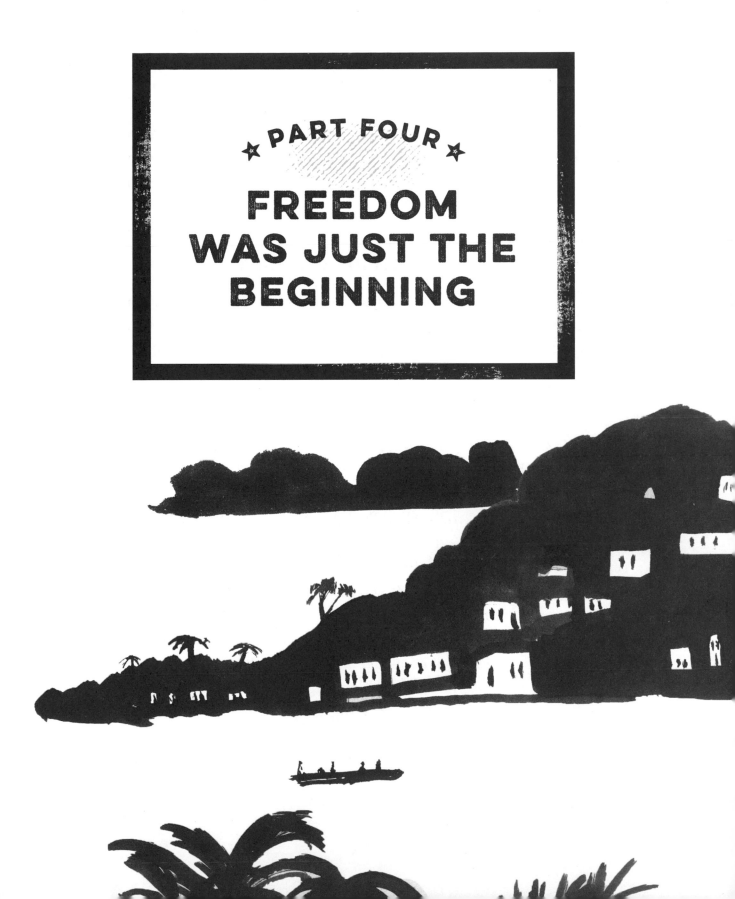

PART FOUR

FREEDOM WAS JUST THE BEGINNING

The American Revolution grew out of radical ideas that all human beings had natural rights, more basic than any that were granted by governments or kings. Did this include slaves? Did they have rights? Many northern churchmen and politicians argued that they did, that slavery was immoral and should be illegal in a nation that championed freedom. Most southerners disagreed.

ABOLITION IN THE NORTH

In the north, the voices of abolition won the day. Vermont's constitution abolished slavery in 1777. In 1780, Pennsylvania passed the first state law for gradual abolition. It freed no slave in 1780. But slaves' children born after March 1, 1780, became "indentured servants," bound to work for their master for no wages, until age twenty-eight, then freed.

In Massachusetts, the courts declared slavery unconstitutional in 1783, and all slaves were soon freed. By 1784, New Hampshire, Connecticut, and Rhode Island passed gradual emancipation laws similar to Pennsylvania's. New York lawmakers didn't act on gradual abolition until 1799, and New Jersey waited until 1804. Because slaves remained enslaved after these laws were passed, and their children were freed only in adulthood, slavery in the north lingered well into the nineteenth century.

Abolition drew countless runaways to the north, swelling the communities of free blacks, especially in the cities. Congress passed a Fugitive Slave Law in 1793 that strengthened slave owners' efforts to reclaim runaways. Yet a growing number of enslaved men and women took a chance and escaped north, hoping to evade slave catchers.

FREE BUT NOT EQUAL

Most whites, even some who supported abolition, didn't favor equality for African Americans. Many state laws prevented blacks from taking certain jobs, holding office, attending school, and voting.

Some African Americans became skilled craftsmen—blacksmiths, carpenters, and the like. But they often had to take any unskilled job they could find. They were paid less than whites, who resented losing their jobs to black workers. Large-scale riots, as well as violence against individual African Americans, were common.

Denied economic and political power, African Americans turned to one institution that they could control: their churches. They had long practiced their own style of worship, with highly emotional sermons and exuberant hymn-singing, and now they did more. They built their own church buildings and hired their own ministers, sometimes linked to white Protestant churches like the Methodists or Episcopalians. They also formed new denominations. These churches were more than spiritual homes. They provided a safety net for their members, offering financial relief, a social network, and a political voice.

Richard Allen, a slave who bought his own freedom, became the founding minister of the African Methodist Episcopal Church. He used the pulpit to speak out for abolition and civil rights. Jarena Lee, a member of Allen's church, felt the sting of gender discrimination. She longed to become a preacher but was denied the chance in her church. She would not be silenced, though.

Paul Cuffe, born free in Massachusetts, became a wealthy shipowner and trader and worked to improve the economic life of his people. John Kizell, enslaved in Africa as a child, escaped with the British to Nova Scotia, then to Sierra Leone. Speaking the Sherbo language of his childhood, he worked to end the slave trade in Africa.

These three men and one woman realized that freedom was just the beginning of the long road to equality. Yet they had the courage to begin the journey.

CHAPTER TEN

PAUL CUFFE

(1759–1817)

Paul Cuffe, twenty years old, cast off from the dock at Westport, Massachusetts, and set sail for Nantucket Island, eight hours and fifty miles away. This was his fourth voyage to the island. His small open boat was filled with goods to sell, but he had to watch for British ships and rogue pirates that roamed the coastal waters during these Revolutionary War years.

The wind, waves, and ocean currents were treacherous, and Paul's first solo voyage had ended in disaster when he lost his boat and his cargo in a storm. He built himself a new boat, bought goods on credit, promising to pay when he sold them, and set off again. This time, he met fine weather but foul luck. Pirates attacked him and stole his boat and all his goods.

Paul Cuffe didn't quit. He built another boat and sailed to Nantucket a third time. Pirates gave chase. But night was coming on, and Paul escaped, only to strike a rock that damaged his boat. Still, he didn't give up.

This day, his fourth try, was all smooth sailing. He reached Nantucket, sold his goods for a tidy profit, and cast off for Westport.

Perhaps after a few such trips, he could build a larger boat, carry more cargo, and sail to far-off ports as captain of his own ship.

It was not to be, or not quite yet. Pirates attacked him again, stole his money, and beat him. Bruised and aching, Paul sailed home.

At least he still had his boat.

"ROBBED OF EVERY THING, HE RETURNED HOME PENNYLESS BUT NOT DISCOURAGED."

—Memoirs of the Life of Paul Cuffee

Paul grew up surrounded by the sea, on the tiny, windswept island of Cuttyhunk, off the coast of Massachusetts. His mother was a Wampanoag Indian, and her ten children were born free into a close-knit Indian community. Paul's father, Cuffe (pronounced KUFF-ee) Slocum, enslaved in Africa and freed as a young man in Cuttyhunk, taught his sons boatbuilding and sailing. When Paul was seven, the family bought a farm and moved to the mainland.

Cuffe Slocum died a few years later, and Paul adopted his father's African name to become Paul Cuffe (sometimes spelled *Cuff* or *Cuffee*). Paul and his brothers divided up the family farm and supported their mother and sisters, but their land, filled with rocky soil and battered by harsh weather, didn't provide enough income. So when Paul turned fourteen, he went to sea.

A career at sea was a good choice for men of color. Each crew member had assigned duties and was judged by his skills, not his race. Life aboard ship was an integrated, fairly equal-opportunity environment.

Young Paul Cuffe joined the crew of a whaling ship for his first seafaring adventure. New England whalers traveled round the world hunting the largest mammals on earth. As Paul swabbed the deck and climbed the rigging, he dreamed of becoming Captain Cuffe.

His next voyages took him to the West Indies, where he witnessed the cruelest sort of slavery. Men and women working on sugar plantations often met an early death through overwork, starvation, and disease. Plantation owners found it cheaper to buy new slaves than to treat them humanely. Cuffe, still a teenager, vowed to try to end slavery one day.

When the American Revolution began in 1775, Britain set up a blockade to prevent American ships from leaving or entering U.S. ports. Cuffe's captain tried to run the blockade, but his ship was captured and the crew was given a choice: join the British navy or go to prison. Cuffe and his shipmates chose prison. After three months, the British prisons grew overcrowded, and the crew was released. Paul returned to the family farm, but the sea drew him back.

He tried his luck sailing his own small boat to Nantucket. After his early run-ins with pirates, he built a larger boat, hired a seaman to sail with him, and ventured south to trade in Connecticut. Cuffe managed to avoid pirates, but he didn't avoid the talk of freedom and equality the Patriots were fighting for.

> ## "AN OLD FRIEND . . . IN THE SHORT SPACE OF TWO WEEKS TAUGHT HIM THE FIRST PRINCIPLES OF NAVIGATION."
>
> —Memoirs of the
> Life of Paul Cuffee

PROTEST BY PETITION

He had grown up hearing "No taxation without representation." White Patriots protested that since they couldn't elect members of Parliament in Britain, they wouldn't be bound by British tax laws. In 1780, five years into the war, Paul Cuffe, his brother John, and five other free

African Americans used the same argument. As property owners, they had to pay taxes. But as African Americans, they couldn't vote. So they sent a formal petition to the Massachusetts legislature:

> *The petition of several poor Negroes & mollatoes [mixed race] . . . Humbly Sheweth—That we being chiefly of the African Extract . . . are not allowed the privilege of freemen of the state having no vote or Influence in the Election of those that Tax us. . . . Most honourable court we Humbley beseech they would to take this into consideration and sit [set] us aside from Paying tax or taxes.*

Their petition was turned down; they still owed their taxes.

The Cuffe brothers tried another tactic. They sent another petition to the county court claiming their rights as Wampanoag Indians, "and by law not the subject of Taxation." This didn't work either. They spent a few hours in jail, and their taxes were still due.

"WE BEING CHIEFLY OF THE AFRICAN EXTRACT . . . ARE NOT ALLOWED THE PRIVILEGE OF FREEMEN OF THE STATE HAVING NO VOTE OR INFLUENCE IN THE ELECTION OF THOSE THAT TAX US."

Cuffe's court case dragged on for more than a year, until a judge ruled that the voting issue should be decided by lawmakers, not a judge. He agreed to drop the case if the Cuffes paid a small tax, which they did. Two years later, in 1783, the Cuffe brothers won the day, when the Massachusetts legislature passed a law giving male African American property owners the right to vote, on the same terms as white men.

CHARTING A COURSE TO PROSPERITY

Paul Cuffe married Alice Pequit, a Wampanoag Indian, when he was twenty-four, and they eventually had seven children. Cuffe made his fortune at sea. He built a schooner to fish the waters off Newfoundland and bought a whaling ship. Eventually, he sold those boats and built an even larger cargo ship in his own shipyard. He bought a larger farm in Westport for his growing family. He also bought a water-powered flour mill and a water-pumping windmill.

Through the years, Cuffe gave jobs to his brothers and sisters, their spouses and children, as well as his own children. He fulfilled his boyhood dream and became a ship's captain, sailing with African American and Native American crews, carrying goods from New England to New York, Philadelphia, and farther south.

> ### "PAUL CUFF [IS] THE OWNER AND MASTER OF A FINE SHIP. HE IS A MAN . . . WORTH 20,000 DOLLARS . . . AND HAS HIS FAMILY SETTLED ABOUT HIM WHO ARE ALSO MUCH RESPECTED."
>
> —John Parrish

In 1796, when Cuffe's ship arrived for the first time in Maryland, a slave state, "the people were filled with astonishment and alarm. A vessel owned and commanded by a person of colour, and manned with a crew of the same complexion, was unprecedented and surprising." People worried

> ### "A VESSEL OWNED AND COMMANDED BY A PERSON OF COLOUR, AND MANNED WITH A CREW OF THE SAME COMPLEXION, WAS UNPRECEDENTED AND SURPRISING."
>
> —Memoirs of the Life of Paul Cuffee

that such a crew might "excite a destructive revolt" by enslaved and free blacks, and officials tried to prevent the ship from docking. But Paul Cuffe persisted. All his documents were in order and he stepped ashore.

Over the next few days, he and his crew won over the hostile townspeople, and Cuffe even dined with prominent white families. The captain and his crew returned to Delaware and Maryland many times, and the Wilmington Abolition Society proclaimed that "their conduct has always furnished strong testimony in favour of the belief that the descendants of Africa are not inferior to Europeans or Americans in moral or intellectual capacity."

Paul Cuffe spent his life proving that this was so.

QUAKER CONNECTION

Paul Cuffe was a deeply religious man, as well as a good businessman. On Cuttyhunk Island, he and his family had attended meetings of the Quakers, the popular name for the Religious Society of Friends. Quakers forbade their members from owning slaves, worked to abolish slavery, and welcomed African Americans—though they sat in the back of the meetinghouse.

One Sunday, after Cuffe stood to give an inspiring message, a white man beckoned him to come forward and sit beside him. Cuffe refused and sat down again with the African Americans. When the Westport Quakers built a new meetinghouse, Cuffe donated half of the cost of the building.

From their earliest days, Quaker schools educated girls as well as boys. Cuffe had had no formal schooling and was determined to educate his sons and daughters. Westport had no primary school, and local children were taught at home or not at all, or traveled to neighboring towns. In 1797, Cuffe approached the townspeople about building a school. No one was interested. Some believed education, beyond Bible reading, was not necessary. Others pled poverty. Still others were uneasy about black and white children attending school together.

"Paul set himself to work in earnest, and had a suitable [school] house built on his own ground." A teacher was hired, and his neighbors, suddenly interested, sent their children to Cuff's School, as it was called.

Cuffe believed that education would expand opportunities for African American children and prove that blacks were not inferior to whites. Also, children working and playing together might eliminate some of the racism that people of color faced every day.

REACHING OUT TO AFRICA

Paul Cuffe had achieved fortune and even fame by his fiftieth birthday and could have retired. But he was a creative, resourceful man, looking to help not only himself and his family but all people of color. Northern states were abolishing slavery by the early 1800s, but it was expanding in the south.

In 1808, the U.S. Congress passed a law ending the slave trade. Transporting enslaved Africans to America was now illegal. Even so, American ships continued to smuggle slaves into southern ports. Cuffe knew that as long as African

> "PAUL SET HIMSELF TO WORK IN EARNEST... AND THE SCHOOL [WAS] OPEN TO ALL WHO PLEASED TO SEND THEIR CHILDREN."
>
> —Memoirs of the Life of Paul Cuffee

"A PERSON LIKE PAUL CUFFE WOULD MOST UNQUESTIONABLY BE A DESIRABLE ACCESSION TO THE POPULATION OF SIERRA LEONE."

—*Zachary Macaulay, Governor of Sierra Leone*

tribesmen were willing to sell captives from enemy tribes, Americans would buy them. What was needed were new ways for Africans to trade and prosper—ways that would be as profitable as the slave trade, but moral and humane.

Paul Cuffe thought it over. Why not set up a legal trading network between Africa and the United States and encourage African Americans to settle in Africa? They could escape the discrimination that they suffered in the United States. They could return to the land of their ancestors, carrying ideas of self-government they had learned in America. They could prosper from the untapped African trading market and help end the enslavement of more Africans.

Cuffe was not the first person to propose settling African Americans in Africa. But he had influential friends to call on for support, thanks to his trading business. He knew he was undertaking an enormous task. He wrote: "I feel Very febel and all most Wornout in hard Service and uncapabel of doing much for my Brethren the afferican Race." He continued: "But blessed by god, I am what I am and all that I Can Conceive that god plese to Lay upon me to make an Insterment of me for that Service."

In November 1810, Paul Cuffe, commanding his own ship full of cargo to trade, set off for Africa. As always, he hired a multiracial crew, including three of his nephews. They landed in Freetown, Sierra Leone, where twelve hundred African American freed slaves, now British subjects, had emigrated from Nova Scotia. Dense forests and swaying palm trees contrasted sharply with his native Cuttyhunk. The moist, warm tropical breezes couldn't be more different from the bitter cold winds of New England.

When they came in sight of land, Cuffe's ship's log simply says, "The Dust of Africa lodged on our Riging." On their first day in Freetown, he wrote: "Caught 1 Dolfin and many sukerfish So We had an Excellent fish Dinner for the first time Since We Sailed from America." But in Freetown's harbor, he saw illegal slave ships that had been captured by the British navy, and many of them were American.

The continuing American slave trade was just the first of Cuffe's disappointments. The British governor of Freetown, wary of foreign competitors, wouldn't let Cuffe sell his cargo. After much negotiation, the governor allowed him to sell some of it. But white merchants in town didn't offer him a fair price. So Cuffe sold to the black Freetown settlers and told them about his plan to build trade with America and resettle African Americans in Sierra Leone.

Cuffe praised the churches and six schools that the black settlers had built in Freetown. Perhaps thinking of his five daughters, he made special mention of a school for thirty girls, "Which Was a Pleasing prospect in Sierra Leone."

But he was not pleased to see how much the settlers liked their liquor, and he wrote: "The industery on their farmes are too much neglected." A few white Englishmen ran the colony, and Cuffe saw that the black settlers needed to "become mannegers of themselves and when they become thus quallified to Carry on Commerce I See no Reason why they may not become a Nation to be . . . numbered among the historians nations of the World."

To begin this process, Cuffe and twelve leading settlers formed the Friendly Society, a business cooperative. The group agreed to set prices and trade freely within Africa. With a strong local network, Cuffe thought, the native Africans could sell their local products—sugar-cane, timber, coffee, cotton, rice, and native crafts—rather than slaves. Cuffe had bigger plans, too, and looked for sites to build lumber and cotton mills.

As he prepared to leave for America, he received a letter from the African Institution, a group of English abolitionists in London. They wrote that the British government had granted Cuffe a license to trade in England as well as Sierra Leone, and the group wanted to meet him in person. This license could set his master plan in motion.

TO ENGLAND

Off to England he sailed. One of his nephews remained in Freetown, so Cuffe took a young African aboard. When they arrived, a British news-paper reported:

On the first of the present month of August, 1811, a vessel arrived at Liverpool, with a cargo from Sierra Leone, the owner, master, mate, and whole crew of which are free Negroes. The master, who is also owner, is the son of an American Slave, and is said to be very well skilled both in trade and navigation, as well as to be of a very pious and moral character. It must have been a strange and animating spectacle to see this free and enlightened African entering, as an independent trader, with his black crew, into that port which was so lately the nidus [spider's nest] of the Slave Trade.

Cuffe was warmly welcomed, but his crew was not. Two of his sailors, exploring the city, were captured by a "press gang"—a group of ruffians who "sold" unwary sailors to the British navy. Cuffe rushed to their aid, declared the two sailors American citizens, and secured their release. The young African was also seized and "pressed" into the navy. Appeals by Cuffe and his Liverpool friends failed, for the English claimed that the young man was a British subject. Cuffe's influential contacts in London intervened and the young man was released.

The English admired Paul Cuffe. One wrote: "His person is tall, well formed and athletic; his deportment conciliating, yet dignified and serious." People also noted that he "dressed in the Quaker style, in a drab-coloured suit, and wears a large flapped white hat."

> "THE BRIG TRAVELLER ... IS PERHAPS THE FIRST VESSEL THAT EVER REACHED EUROPE, ENTIRELY OWNED AND NAVIGATED BY NEGROES."
>
> —The Times of London

Cuffe met with abolitionists, members of Parliament, a government committee headed by the king's brother—and he impressed them all. One man, commenting on his plans for a trading network, said, "He seems like a man made on purpose for the business."

The British government approved Paul Cuffe's plan for American trade with their African colonies. All was proceeding smoothly. But when his ship, filled with English goods, landed in Freetown, English officials again tried to stop him from selling his cargo. They had him followed wherever he went.

Cuffe got caught in the middle of a dispute between the governor and the settlers. He realized he couldn't oppose the governor or he could lose his trading license. Cuffe wrote: "When men are like Lions We must be Carefull how we git our hands in their mouths and if We Should Chance to We must Endeavour to git out the Best Way of prudence."

"HIS PERSON IS TALL, WELL FORMED AND ATHLETIC; HIS DEPORTMENT CONCILIATING, YET DIGNIFIED AND SERIOUS."

For his return to America, Cuffe took three apprentice sailors on board from Freetown. Enroute, he showed his playful side, not often expressed in his ships' logs and business letters. He began to teach the boys the science of navigation using traditional folk rhymes:

If the Wind Come before the Rain
Lower the topsails & hoist them again
If the Rain Comes before the Wind
Lower the topsails and take them in.

A ROCKY PATH OF PEACEFULNESS

When Paul Cuffe arrived back in Massachusetts in April 1812, after a seventeen-month absence, U.S. Customs officials seized his ship. Britain and America were on the brink of war, Congress had outlawed trade with Great Britain, and Cuffe's ship was filled with British goods. He needed a pardon from the secretary of the treasury, Albert Gallatin, to retrieve his cargo. He went to Washington, D.C., to meet with Gallatin and President James Madison to discuss the matter.

Quakers don't use titles but address everyone by his or her first name. Cuffe said, "James, I have been put to much trouble, and have been abused. . . . I have come here for thy protection." Madison ordered Cuffe's cargo restored to him. Then the president asked for his advice about using force against the illegal slave traders. Cuffe, a Quaker pacifist, replied that he "Was travelling in a parth of peacabulness." He couldn't support violence.

On his way home from Washington, he experienced the highs and lows of being Paul Cuffe. The low came in Maryland, when he was denied a table in a tavern and ordered to eat in the kitchen with the slaves. He found another tavern instead, "not as I thought myself better than the Servants, but from the nature of the Cause." The highs came in Philadelphia and New York, where he gave speeches about his African trading plan to admiring crowds.

But even in the north, he faced ridicule. Sometimes he responded with a quick wit. On a New York street, two Methodist preachers asked him if he spoke English. He answered, "There Was a Part [of English] I did not understand that of one Brother professor [Christian] makeing merchandize of and holding in Bondage their Brother [Christian] professor. this parte I Should be glad they Would Clear up to me." The two preachers hurried off without another word.

RETURN TO AFRICA

The War of 1812 kept Cuffe at home for three years. In 1815, with peace restored, Cuffe finally set sail for Sierra Leone with thirty-eight African Americans eager to settle there. He had hoped for more settlers and asked them to pay for their own passage. Only one of them did, and Cuffe paid for the rest. He also paid for axes, hoes, a plow, a wagon, and sawmill parts to help them get started in their new home.

When Cuffe reached Freetown, he was annoyed but not surprised when British officials charged him high duties on his cargo. But he was pleased that the Friendly Society, the business cooperative, was thriving. The new African American settlers received their promised farmland, and by the time Cuffe left, "they were in high Spirits." Except one man complained about taking time from farming to serve on a jury. Cuffe reminded the man that "he Complained in America because he was deprived of these liberties and then murmured because he was thus Called upon." Cuffe told him, "Go and fill thy Seat and do as well as thou Canst."

> "A SOUND UNDERSTANDING, UNITED WITH ENERGY AND PERSEVERANCE, SEEMS TO HAVE RENDERED HIM CAPABLE OF SURMOUNTING DIFFICULTIES WHICH WOULD HAVE DISCOURAGED AN ORDINARY MIND."
>
> —Memoirs of the Life of Paul Cuffee

Cuffe took note of the American slave ships he saw in Sierra Leone:

Just arrived Captured . . . the schooner Rebecca of New York. . . . Also there was 3 brigs and 3 schooners taken and Condemned at Sierra Leone in the course of 2 months. These Vessels (it was said) was found guilty of Carrying on the Slave trade.

This list caused a furor when it was published in a dozen newspapers in New York and reprinted in other papers from Washington, D.C., to Boston. Cuffe was fulfilling the vow he had made when he sailed to the West Indies as a teenager: to fight peacefully for the end of slavery.

Paul Cuffe lived just one more year, and though his plan for closer American and African trade didn't come to pass, he achieved something more important. By his own example, he showed that free people of color could live and thrive in a multicultural society in America.

CHAPTER ELEVEN

JOHN KIZELL

(ca. 1760–after 1830)

Nighttime in an African village. Among the mud huts with thatched roofs, a group of boys sat listening to an old man tell stories about animals acting like humans and devils haunting the jungle. The boys laughed at the comic tales and shivered with fright at the scary ones. Tonight, a visitor joined their circle: the nephew of the village chief.

Suddenly, screams ripped through the night and a band of warriors burst into the village, waving swords and guns. Amid the shrieks and gunshots, men lay moaning, bleeding, and dying. Others ran into the jungle. The young visitor didn't know where to run. As he tried to dodge the slashing swords, he was knocked to the ground and dragged away into the darkness.

When the boy's father, the chief of his own village, heard the terrible news, he offered to exchange three slaves of his own in return for his son. The kidnappers scoffed at the offer. They wanted to sell the boy to foreign slave traders. Their customs allowed them to sell only criminals and witches, so they invented cruel lies about the boy, called him a witch, judged him guilty, and sold him to white men. He was marched in chains to the seacoast and shipped across the ocean.

Since the 1600s, tribes in West Africa had been selling men, women, and children to European and American slave traders. They received payment in liquor, tobacco, and guns.

One such captive stood at a slave auction in Charleston, South Carolina, in 1773. He was just thirteen and small for his age, not a good prospect for backbreaking plantation fieldwork. Esther Kysell, a German widow, bought the boy, called him John, and set him to work in her Charleston inn.

> **"I HAVE SEEN A MAN DELIVER UP ANOTHER HE HAS CALLED HIS FRIEND, FOR A LITTLE RUM, TOBACCO, OR CLOTH! WHOLE FAMILIES HAVE BEEN SOLD BY THESE KIND FRIENDS."**
>
> —*John Kizell*

As John ran errands through the busy city, he saw ships from foreign parts arriving in Charleston Harbor, carrying goods from Europe and the West Indies as well as captives from Africa. Half the faces he saw in the city were black, nearly all of them enslaved. African American men worked as boatmen, fishermen, carpenters, and butchers. Women sold goods at stalls in the marketplace.

> **"[CHARLESTON SLAVES] DID NOT ACT LIKE SLAVES. THEY WERE NOT SERVILE; THEY WERE PROUD, HAUGHTY, SELF-CONFIDENT."**
>
> —*Philip Morgan*

A BLACK LOYALIST

As John Kizell began to learn English, he heard talk of liberty for the thirteen American colonies. But not for the enslaved. He heard that the

British offered to free Patriot slaves who became Loyalists. When British troops captured Charleston in May 1780, twenty-year-old John Kizell seized his chance. He joined a British force of eleven hundred Black and White Loyalists and tramped through the wilderness of North and South Carolina, battling malaria, dysentery, and Patriot ambushes.

When the Continental army recaptured Charleston in 1782, Kizell saw thousands of freed and runaway slaves in the city trying to escape, for they knew that the Americans would send them back to slavery. Kizell managed to sail away with the British army to British-held New York City, where he lived until the war ended a year later.

HARDSHIP IN NOVA SCOTIA

The victorious Americans wanted their former slaves back—men like John Kizell. But the British refused. They gave the African Americans British Certificates of Freedom and passage to Nova Scotia, a British colony in Canada. John Kizell sailed away with three thousand Black and twenty-seven thousand White Loyalists.

In Nova Scotia, Kizell worked as a servant for a white man. He signed his name to a three-year contract for $60 per year. His wife, Phillis, worked for clothing and food. Two daughters and a son were born to them as they struggled to survive, but they found comfort, community, and spirited preaching and singing in the Baptist church.

After nine years of hardship and discrimination by white officials, the black settlers welcomed John Clarkson, an Englishman,

"[NEVER WOULD THE BRITISH GOVERNMENT] . . . REDUCE THEMSELVES TO THE NECESSITY OF VIOLATING THEIR FAITH TO THE NEGROES."

—*Sir Guy Carlton*

who came to recruit volunteers for a new colony in Sierra Leone, West Africa. He spoke to the Methodists and enlisted Mary and Caesar Perth as well as Boston King and his family. Clarkson spoke at the Baptist church, and John Kizell's family and the entire congregation took up the offer. For many of them, this was a venture into the unknown.

"THE GENERALITY [MAJORITY] OF THE BLACKS . . . SEEMED TO FEEL MORE AT SINGING, THAN THEY DID AT PRAYERS."

—*John Clarkson*

But John Kizell was going home.

He had left Africa when he was thirteen. Now he was thirty-one, a man in his prime. He could read and write English, he had served in the British army, and he had supported his family in desperate circumstances. He knew the language and customs of Africans, Americans, and Englishmen. He sailed to Africa with his wife, his children, and a hopeful heart.

TROUBLES IN FREETOWN

But Kizell and the other Black Loyalists found new sorts of trouble in Freetown, Sierra Leone. They had suffered frigid winters and famine in Nova Scotia. Now they suffered sweltering rainy seasons and tropical diseases. Hundreds of the twelve hundred settlers died in the first few months. The survivors had to clear the jungle for farming, but a white British governor remained in charge.

The settlers had expected to govern themselves. Kizell wrote: "We cannot do any thing of [by] ourselves. It was promised . . . that the Noviscotian and the white should be as one, but instead they have set a parcel of white and mallater [mulatto] boys over us as magistrates." Using protests and petitions, as the American Patriots had done, the former slaves eventually won the right to serve on juries, provide local police services, and elect a local council, which included John Kizell.

Zachary Macaulay, the British governor, had little respect for the council, claiming they were mostly "men of at best dubious character & some of them unquestionably bad." But he admitted that Kizell was one of the "more thinking" settlers. The governor even sent him to England as his representative.

In England, Kizell enrolled his nine-year-old son, George, in school and met members of the Baptist Missionary Society. They admired this man who spoke well and had a good business sense. John Kizell returned to Africa with English goods to sell, paid for by the English Baptists. They told him to keep the profits for himself.

When Kizell arrived home, he learned that France, at war with Britain in Europe, had carried the war to the coast of Africa. French soldiers had attacked Freetown, killing and injuring settlers. The invaders had burned houses, looted shops, stolen money, destroyed furniture and machinery, and killed livestock. Most of Kizell's possessions were gone, but his wife and daughters were safe. He had the English goods to sell to help his family recover their losses. But others had suffered, too, so Kizell shared his profits with his fellow Baptists.

> "IN THE GENEROSITY OF HIS HEART, HE DIVIDED THE PROFITS OF HIS VENTURE AMONG HIS BRETHREN THUS ALLEVIATING THEIR DISTRESS AS FAR AS HE WAS ABLE."
>
> —American Colonization Society

PARTNERS IN TRADE

John Kizell saw a promising future for trade. Freetown needed rice and other goods, and he and two other men built the first sailing sloop in the colony. They named it *Three Friends* and soon brought five tons of rice to Freetown from farming areas nearby. He also joined with Paul Cuffe, the African American ship captain, to form the Friendly Society to develop trade between Africa and America.

Kizell and his family moved from Freetown to nearby Sherbro Island to carry on his trading business. The island, with sandy soil and swampy areas, was not ideal for farming, but it had a good harbor for shipping. Kizell built a Baptist chapel and began to preach in both

English and Sherbro languages. As always, he looked to the resources available to him and made the most of them. Sherbro Island was full of palm trees and he enthusiastically described their virtues:

> This tree is one of the best that grows: I do not know one that is better. It produces the common palm oil, also a fine kind, called nut oil. From its leaves they make excellent lines and rope; and, indeed, it is from this they make all their fishing nets and fishing lines. This tree produces also the palm wine, and the palm cabbage, which is very good food, and eats like a turnip. With the leaves, too, they cover their houses. . . . In the Sherbro, there is plenty of fish and oysters; and plenty of turtles also in their season.

He traveled the rivers of Sierra Leone, his boat loaded with English goods, and returned with rice, coffee, and other produce to sell in Freetown. Through keen insight and hard work, he built a good life for his family. Most men would have been satisfied, but Kizell wanted to do more.

STRADDLING CULTURES

John Kizell was unique among the Black Loyalist settlers. He remembered the Sherbro language from his childhood, and he understood native customs. Africans held "palavers," hours-long conversations, before they struck any deals. Europeans grew impatient with palavers, but Kizell knew this was the only way to do business there. He understood African beliefs in spirits and magic and did not try to change those beliefs. But he did welcome Africans to his Baptist chapel where he preached the Christian gospel.

Kizell's knowledge and talents prompted one African prince to declare that "whenever he looked at Kizell he wished that he too had been made a captive, if through slavery he could but learn the manners, customs and knowledge of other nations."

John Kizell had learned much in North America, including the cruelty of slavery. As a former captive, he knew the personal pain of losing his family. As a Christian, he opposed slavery on moral grounds. As an American, he believed in liberty for all. And as a businessman, he saw the devastating economic consequences when strong young men and women were kidnapped from their villages. Most people were kept poor, while a few grew rich.

By 1808, the slave trade was outlawed, though slavery itself was still legal in the United States. Southerners clamored for more slaves, and illegal American ships kept slave owners well supplied. The British navy patrolled the west African coast to seize slave ships and free the captives, but many ships eluded them.

"HE HAS THE WELFARE OF YOU AND HIS COUNTRY VERY EARNESTLY AT HEART."

MAKE FARMS, NOT WAR

In 1810, John Kizell and the English governor of Sierra Leone, Edward Columbine, worked together on a plan to replace the slave trade with farming and trading in native African villages. Black men would be in charge, and all profits would go to the villagers. Kizell, an ideal spokesman, arranged to meet with local chiefs and tribal kings to acquire land for the project.

Laden with traditional gifts of rum and tobacco, Kizell traveled to the interior of Sierra Leone. He carried a letter from Governor Columbine that described Kizell as "one of yourselves; and he has the welfare of you and his country very earnestly at heart."

The first chief he met liked the plan of exchanging slave trading for farming, but wouldn't commit to any action. At Kizell's second stop, the young people sided with him, but slave traders opposed him. In any case, the chief wouldn't act unless the king and all the chiefs of the region agreed to the plan.

"I TOLD THEM THAT THE BLOOD OF THEIR PEOPLE CRIED AGAINST THEM, AND THAT GOD HAD HEARD IT."

Kizell traveled further and met many headmen. "I told them that the blood of their people cried against them, and that God had heard it. . . . For a little rum and tobacco they allowed their people to be carried off, and said nothing."

He met a queen who complained that he had not brought her enough rum. He replied that "the Governor did not send me to blind her eyes, but to open them; and to persuade her no longer to sell her people." The women in the village "clapped their hands for joy . . . [and] the young people said, 'the old people knew that *they* could not be sold, but that it was the young people who must be sold.'" The queen promised to meet Kizell again, but she never arrived for the second meeting. Kizell was outraged by this insult.

"'THE OLD PEOPLE KNEW THAT *THEY* COULD NOT BE SOLD, BUT THAT IT WAS THE YOUNG PEOPLE WHO MUST BE SOLD.'"

As he traveled from place to place, slave traders turned some chiefs against him, saying he had come to make war against them. "At one time they were so violent, I thought they would have beat me." John Kizell finally met the king of Sherbro, who offered one more excuse. He would not deal with a common black man like Kizell, but only with the governor or a white official.

> "THEY INQUIRED, 'IF YOU COME TO STOP THE SLAVE TRADE, WHAT SHALL WE DO FOR A LIVING?' I ANSWERED, 'YOU AND YOUR PEOPLE . . . MUST ALL WORK, AS OTHER PEOPLE DO.'"
>
> —*John Kizell*

The king and the chiefs claimed that they wanted to end the slave trade, but Kizell saw that wasn't true. Africans accepted slavery as a normal part of life. Kizell had heard the same argument in America: slavery was the natural order of things.

Though his diplomatic mission failed, John Kizell didn't give up. He would look for another way to prove to Africans that prosperity was possible without trading in slaves.

BRINGING AFRICAN AMERICANS TO AFRICA

John Kizell believed that African Americans, committed to democracy and abolition, could show the African slave traders a different way to live. He turned to the American Colonization Society (ACS), a group that wanted to settle African Americans in Africa. African American leaders realized that the ACS only wanted to get rid of free blacks. Senator Henry Clay of Kentucky endorsed the plan "to rid our country of a useless and pernicious, if not dangerous portion of our population." Dangerous, because the growing population of

> "AFRICA IS THE LAND OF BLACK MEN AND TO AFRICA THEY MUST AND WILL COME."

free blacks inspired many people to try to escape to freedom.

John Kizell was willing to work with the ACS, though, for Africa's sake. He said, "Africa is the land of black men and to Africa they must and will come. . . . They have not forfeited a right to the inheritance of their forefathers, by being carried by force from their country."

Africa had been the making of John Kizell. He had become a successful businessman, a devout preacher, and a respected diplomat. He wanted others to succeed as he had. He believed that "the greater part of the people of colour, who are now in America, will yet return to Africa."

In March 1820, palm trees swayed in the breeze as John Kizell stood on the sandy beach of Sherbro Island. The ship *Elizabeth* was anchored in the harbor, and he watched eighty-four African Americans and two white ACS agents step onto his native land. Kizell, sixty years old, shed tears of joy as he led the newcomers to his village. He had built African houses for them, made of bamboo poles and mud-plaster walls, with roofs of palm leaves.

"GOD HAS SENT ME HERE AND SET ME DOWN TO MAKE A PLACE FOR MY BRETHREN. . . . YOU CANNOT SEND TOO MANY."

After a dinner of rice and fish cooked in palm oil, the newcomers gathered in Kizell's Baptist chapel. He led a prayer of thanksgiving for the African Americans' safe arrival and thanked them for their generous gift of a church bell. Then he spoke to his local congregation—twenty native Africans—in the Sherbro language. He hoped and prayed that all these people could create a new society together, one free of slavery.

John Kizell spoke poetically about his home. Africa is "wide and long. . . . Africa is fertile and healthy," he wrote.

God has sent me here and set me down to make a place for my brethren. . . . You cannot send too many. Let them come down and sit in our valleys, and on our hills, and near our rivers, and all the country will soon break forth into a song. The Sherbro country is full of meat, and fish, and bread and oil, and honey. Send us people to eat them.

One of the ACS agents reported, "No man's heart can be more ardent for the success of our object. And no man in Africa could probably be so useful to us. . . . [John Kizell] owns considerable tracts of land here, and is acknowledged by the natives to be the head man of the country."

Kizell may have been disappointed that only eighty-four settlers arrived from America, but it was a start. He began to work with the ACS agents and settler Daniel Coker, a preacher and former slave, but conflicts quickly arose. The two white

"[JOHN KIZELL] . . . IS ACKNOWLEDGED BY THE NATIVES TO BE THE HEAD MAN OF THE COUNTRY."

agents thought they were in charge, while the black settlers expected to govern themselves. Then malaria and dysentery struck and the agents died, along with twenty-four settlers. The group of eighty-four was reduced to sixty, and Daniel Coker became their leader.

When he and Kizell met with African chiefs to secure land for a settlement, Coker refused to give them rum. He couldn't tolerate the endless palavers. Kizell reported that Coker considered the chiefs "nothing but imposters and blood suckers." The new settlers received no land.

A full-blown feud erupted between Coker and Kizell about how to proceed, and the new settlers left Sherbro Island for Freetown. Before

Coker departed, he pulled down the houses Kizell had built and took back the bell they had donated to his chapel.

SAVING ONE CAPTIVE AT A TIME

John Kizell grew old, but he didn't abandon his battle against slavery. The British navy and a few American navy ships roamed the waters off the coastline. When they captured a slave ship, the captives were freed and settled in villages along the coast.

> "HE IS AN INTELLIGENT MAN . . . AND HAS THE WELFARE OF HIS NATIVE COUNTRY SINCERELY AT HEART. . . . HE APPEARS ALWAYS TO HAVE DISCHARGED HIS DUTY WITH GREAT INTEGRITY AND ADDRESS."
>
> —*Governor Edward Columbine*

In 1825, Kizell, age sixty-five, was appointed superintendent of twenty thousand liberated slaves in his region. It was a difficult job. Many children were "apprenticed" by Africans and sold again into slavery. Kizell found that even freed Africans sometimes bought and sold others, and some Black Loyalist settlers joined in slave trading. The profits were too hard to resist.

But Kizell didn't give up. As one of his last acts before he died, he rescued five boys from a canoe that was headed to a slave ship bound for Cuba. Perhaps John Kizell saw the shadow of his thirteen-year-old self in that canoe. And so he continued, saving one slave—or five—at a time.

CHAPTER TWELVE

RICHARD ALLEN

(1760–1831)

Richard Allen sat upstairs in Philadelphia's St. George's Methodist Church on a Sunday morning. African Americans were not allowed downstairs with the white worshipers, but Allen and Absalom Jones had hatched a plot.

As the white minister intoned a prayer on the main floor, Jones entered the church and knelt in the aisle. When an usher asked Jones to move upstairs, he refused. The usher asked again. Jones replied that he would move when the prayer was over, but the usher forced him to his feet.

At that point, Richard Allen stood up with everyone else in the balcony. Then he led the entire black congregation down the stairs and out of the church. Their dramatic protest made it clear that Allen and his friends believed that "all men are created equal." Blacks weren't equal in the white Methodist church, so Allen set forth to create a church of their own.

"Negro Richard," so named in his owner's records, spent his first seven years in Philadelphia, where his parents worked as house slaves. When his family was sold to Stokeley Sturgis, a farmer in Delaware, young Richard went to work in the fields of wheat, corn, and flax. Sturgis fell on hard times and, to pay his debts, he wrenched Richard's family apart. His mother and three of his siblings were sold, while Richard, one brother, and one sister remained with Sturgis. There are no records of his father's fate.

When Richard was seventeen, he heard a traveling Methodist minister preach. He must have heard Christian sermons before, but none touched him so deeply. Richard wrote: "All of a sudden my dungeon shook, my chains flew off, and glory to God, I cried. My soul was filled." Richard joined the Methodists, urged his friends to seek religion—and a future preacher was born.

"ALL OF A SUDDEN MY DUNGEON SHOOK, MY CHAINS FLEW OFF, AND GLORY TO GOD, I CRIED."

A PATH TO FREEDOM

Religion gave Richard more than spiritual strength. It gave him a path to freedom. Richard described his owner, Stokeley Sturgis, as "what the world called a good master. He was more like a father to his slaves than any thing else. He was a very tender, humane man." Sturgis gave Richard and his brother John permission to attend prayer meetings twice a month.

Sturgis's friends warned him that religion would ruin his slaves, making them feel important and giving them an excuse not to work. But Richard and John worked harder than ever, sometimes even skipping prayer meetings. Sturgis told his friends "he was convinced that religion made slaves better and not worse." He also boasted of "their honesty and industry." The first stage of Richard's freedom campaign was complete: he had convinced Sturgis that religion was good for slaves.

Next, Richard asked if he could invite Methodist preachers to Sturgis's house. The slaves were enthusiastic, the white man merely tolerant. But Sturgis let the prayer meetings continue in his kitchen, then in his parlor.

One night, Richard invited Freeborn Garrettson to preach. Garrettson, a white farmer turned minister, had freed his own slaves. That night, he preached on these words from the Bible: "Thou art weighed in the balance, and art found wanting." Garrettson spoke straight to Sturgis and made it clear that his sins lay in owning slaves. Sturgis got the message. He was an old man and feared divine judgment when he died. He offered Richard the chance to buy his freedom.

So began the third stage of Richard's freedom campaign. He signed a contract in January 1780 to pay Sturgis $2,000 for his freedom within five years, with $400 due each year. Sturgis gave Richard a written pass that allowed him to travel freely and earn his own money.

> ## "SLAVERY IS A BITTER PILL, NOTWITHSTANDING WE HAD A GOOD MASTER."
> —*Richard Allen*

WORKING TO BUY FREEDOM

Richard had never had to find work when he was enslaved, nor had he earned a penny for his labors. But his will was strong and so was his body. He found a job chopping wood, and at the end of the first day his hands were blistered and sore. He soon developed callused hands that could swing an ax day after day.

Richard hauled bricks in a brick-yard. He worked as a stonemason and a butcher. He drove a wagon carrying salt to American troops fighting the Revolutionary War. As he went from place to place, he preached to people he met. Traveling and preaching brought him "many happy seasons in meditation and prayer," he wrote.

"WHEN I LEFT MY MASTER'S HOUSE I KNEW NOT WHAT TO DO, NOT BEING USED TO HARD WORK."

—*Richard Allen*

Richard worked with a determination he would display all his life. He paid his first installment to Sturgis six months early and made his final payment eighteen months ahead of schedule. He received his legal manumission—freedom—papers on August 17, 1783.

I Do hereby . . . manumit Exonerate Release and for Ever Discharge and set at full Liberty the Said Negro Man named Richard quitting all Claim that I . . . might have to him.

—*Stokeley Sturgis*

Freedman "Negro Richard" renamed himself Richard Allen. He never explained where the name came from. Perhaps he wanted to honor William Allen, a well-known judge and supporter of the 1780 Pennsylvania abolition law that gradually ended slavery.

SEEKING HIS AFRICAN BRETHREN

By 1783, the American Revolution was over and Richard Allen was free. For the next three years, he traveled through town and country in New Jersey, Pennsylvania, Maryland, and Delaware, preaching the

Methodist message. Allen received no pay. When he ran out of funds or needed new clothes, he worked for a farmer or a tradesman, then went on his way.

Richard Allen joined white preachers and even a bishop on their travels around the middle Atlantic states. He met people of many social classes and religions. When Methodist churchmen in Philadelphia invited Allen to preach in February 1786, he accepted. He intended to stay a week or two, but he stayed for forty-five years, the rest of his life.

Thirteen hundred African Americans, most of them free, lived in Philadelphia, the largest and most prosperous city in America. But racism infected their daily lives. Jobs and housing, even squalid housing, were hard to find, and public schools didn't admit black children.

In Philadelphia, Allen formed a plan that would grow through the decades. He had preached mostly to whites, but now he turned to his

> **"I ... PREACHED ON SABBATH DAY TO A LARGE CONGREGATION OF DIFFERENT PERSUASIONS, AND MY DEAR LORD WAS WITH ME, AND I BELIEVE THERE WERE MANY SOULS CUT TO THE HEART, AND WERE ADDED TO THE MINISTRY."**
>
> —*Richard Allen*

own people. As he described it, "I soon saw a large field open in seeking and instructing my African brethren, who had been a long forgotten people and few of them attended public worship."

Allen's preaching didn't support him and he had to make a living. He started a chimney-sweeping business. Cleaning soot-filled chimneys was dirty, unskilled work, the sort of job available to African Americans. Over the years, he worked as a shoemaker and a grocer and bought several houses which he rented out, and a farm near Philadelphia.

As Allen established himself in his new home city, he met Absalom Jones, an African American preacher who became his mentor. Jones, fourteen years older than Allen, had purchased his wife's freedom, then his own. The two men formed the Free African Society (FAS), which offered financial support to widows, orphans, and those who were ill. The FAS was open to all who paid dues and lived "an orderly and sober life." Free blacks proudly embraced their heritage, and the word *African* appeared in the name of many early organizations.

Jones and Allen also founded an African Lodge of the Freemasons, following the lead of Prince Hall in Boston. Such organizations not only created a sense of community among blacks, but they also worked to gain respect from white society.

YELLOW-FEVER EPIDEMIC

In 1793, an epidemic of yellow fever, a disease carried by mosquitoes, broke out in Philadelphia. Victims suffered headaches, chills, sharp chest pains, even madness, and many died within a few days. During the worst of the epidemic, hundreds of people died every day.

Wealthy people with country homes fled the city. Middle-class citizens with relatives living elsewhere left as well. Poor people with nowhere to go suffered the most. Some doctors believed that African Americans were immune to yellow fever. (This was untrue. Richard Allen was one who caught the disease, but he survived.) A call went out from the mayor to Richard Allen and Absalom Jones: could the black community help nurse the sick? They could—and they could do much more.

For several months during that terrible summer, African

> "WE HAVE SUFFERED **EQUALLY** WITH THE WHITES. . . . FEW HAVE BEEN THE WHITES THAT **PAID ATTENTION** TO US, WHILE THE COLOURED PERSONS WERE ENGAGED IN OTHERS' SERVICE."
>
> —*Richard Allen*

Americans buried the dead, who were often left lying in the streets. They rescued orphans whose families had died, and they nursed the sick and dying. Later in the fall, as the weather cooled and mosquitoes died, the epidemic ended and people returned to the city.

Philadelphia's mayor praised the work of the African Americans:

"SURELY OUR TASK WAS HARD; YET THROUGH MERCY WE WERE ENABLED TO GO ON."

—*Richard Allen*

Having, during the prevalence of the late malignant disorder, had almost daily opportunities of seeing the conduct of Absalom Jones and Richard Allen, and the people employed by them to bury the dead—I with cheerfulness give this testimony of my approbation [approval] of their proceedings. . . . Their diligence, attention, and decency of deportment, afforded me, at the time, much satisfaction.

—MATTHEW CLARKSON, *Mayor.*
Philadelphia, Jan. 23d, 1794.

But Mathew Carey, a printer, published an account accusing black workers of looting, robbing, and abusing fever victims. Carey's pamphlet strengthened many white people's scorn for African Americans.

FIGHTING INJUSTICE WITH HIS PEN

Richard Allen took up his pen to defend his people. He and Absalom Jones published a pamphlet called A *Narrative of the Proceedings of the Black People, During the Late Awful Calamity in Philadelphia, in the Year 1793: and a Refutation of Some Censures, Thrown Upon Them in Some Late Publications*. Allen and Jones applied to the federal government for a copyright to protect their work from distortion or illegal use—the first U.S. copyright granted to African American authors.

The *Narrative* expressed Allen and Jones's outrage at Carey's accusations, but it also did much more. The authors named specific volunteers, listed the families they helped, and described what they did for those families. Allen and Jones also noted how much of the city's money they spent for coffins, and hiring horses and carts for burials.

In a separate essay included in the *Narrative*, Richard Allen addressed the issue of slavery. To slaveholders he wrote: "If you love your children, if you love your country, if you love the

"WE HAVE MANY UNPROVOKED ENEMIES, WHO BEGRUDGE US THE LIBERTY WE ENJOY, AND ARE GLAD TO HEAR OF ANY COMPLAINT AGAINST OUR COLOUR, BE IT JUST OR UNJUST."

—*Richard Allen*

God of love, clear your hands from slaves, burthen [burden] not your children or your country with them."

To slaves, he hoped that "the favour and love of God dwelling in your hearts . . . will be a consolation in the worst condition you can be in, and no master can deprive you of it."

To free blacks, he warned, "Much depends upon us for the help of our colour—more than many are aware. If we are lazy and idle, the enemies of freedom plead it as a cause why we ought not to be free, and say we are better in a state of servitude."

To white abolitionists, he wrote: "I feel an inexpressible gratitude towards you who have engaged in the cause of the African race. . . . You strive to raise the slave to the dignity of a man; you take our children by the hand to lead them in the path of virtue, by your care of our education."

Richard Allen wrote pamphlets, broadsides (one-page essays), and newspaper articles to spread his ideas. When George Washington died, Allen preached a eulogy sermon and printed it in the *Philadelphia Gazette*. Allen focused not on Washington's military and political triumphs but on the fact that he freed all his slaves in his will—the only slave-owning Founding Father to do so.

"MUCH DEPENDS UPON US FOR THE HELP OF OUR COLOUR—MORE THAN MANY ARE AWARE."

We, my friends, have particular cause to bemoan our loss. . . . He whose wisdom the nations revered thought we had a right to liberty. Unbiased by the popular opinion of the state [Virginia] in which is the memorable Mount Vernon—he dared to do his duty, and wipe off the only stain with which man could ever reproach him.

BUILDING AN AFRICAN AMERICAN CHURCH

Richard Allen made his mark as a community organizer and writer, but his dream was to establish an independent African American church. St. George's Methodist Church had allowed him to preach at 5 a.m. Later in the day, he could preach in people's homes or in the open air, but not in church. Finally, Richard Allen and Absalom Jones rebelled against this second-class treatment. They staged their walkout in St. George's Church.

"HE [WASHINGTON] DARED TO DO HIS DUTY, AND WIPE OFF THE ONLY STAIN WITH WHICH MAN COULD EVER REPROACH HIM."

Most of the protesters, including Absalom Jones, wanted nothing more to do with the Methodists. They accepted the Episcopal Church's offer to form St. Thomas's African Episcopal Church. Richard Allen was asked to be the minister, but he refused. He was a Methodist through and through. So Absalom Jones took the job.

Allen remained loyal to the Methodists because they "were the first people that brought glad tidings to the coloured people. . . . All other denominations preached so high-flown that we were not able to comprehend their doctrine." Methodists spoke the "plain and simple gospel" that "suits best for any people, the unlearned can understand, and the learned are sure to understand."

"WE ALL WENT OUT OF THE CHURCH IN A BODY, AND THEY WERE NO MORE PLAGUED WITH US IN THE CHURCH."

—*Richard Allen*

But Allen wanted more than plain-speaking sermons. He wanted a church where African American ministers could preach at any hour, and that black congregations could run themselves. The church he wanted would be separate from white people—both well-meaning groups and hostile groups.

Richard Allen bought a vacant lot with his own money, hired a team of mules, and moved a wooden blacksmith shop onto the lot. This became the first Bethel Church, officially known as the African Methodist Episcopal (AME) Church. It was dedicated on July 29, 1794, with twenty-one members. The churchmen at St. George's Methodist Church were not happy with Allen's "declaration of independence." For twenty-two years, Allen and Bethel Church fought with the white Methodists over who could lead services and who owned the property.

> ## "I COULD NOT BE ANY THING ELSE BUT A METHODIST."
> —*Richard Allen*

Richard Allen took the case to court. In 1816, the court agreed that the AME Church was an independent corporation and white Methodists had no legal claim to it. By then, Bethel Church had grown to one thousand members and was still expanding, as more AME Churches sprang up in other cities.

Richard Allen knew that his church could be a powerful political instrument for African Americans. Several slave revolts erupted in the south during Allen's lifetime, and race riots broke out in the north. Allen had known slavery and discrimination, but he insisted on nonviolence. He began his autobiography with a Bible quote: "Mark [see] the perfect man, and behold the upright: for the end [goal] of that man is peace." He believed that African Americans

> ## "[THEY] MIGHT DENY US THEIR NAME [OF METHODISTS], BUT THEY COULD NOT DENY US A SEAT IN HEAVEN."
> —*Richard Allen*

must use the pulpit, the printing press, and the courts of law—not violence—to advance their cause.

AN ELIGIBLE BACHELOR

Richard Allen, a prosperous businessman, respected community leader, and famous preacher, was also an eligible bachelor. He finally chose a wife, Flora, when he was thirty years old. Flora Allen dedicated herself to her husband's work, as she and other churchwomen played an important although subservient role at Bethel Church. Allen preached inspired sermons from the pulpit and church*men* decided how to confront the white Methodists. Meanwhile, Flora Allen and other women taught Sunday school, held prayer meetings at home, raised money, and organized social programs. In 1801, Flora died childless, after eleven years of marriage.

Within a year, Richard married Sarah, a widow, and they had six children together. Sarah had walked out of St. George's Church with Allen, joined Bethel Church, and nursed the sick in the yellow-fever epidemic.

WAS AFRICA THE ANSWER?

Richard Allen had a change of heart around 1815, when he was fifty-five. He came to believe that America would never accept African Americans on equal terms. He began to look to Africa as the answer, and he wasn't alone. Other black leaders had pressed Allen to consider relocating African Americans to Africa. There they could escape from racism, govern themselves, and bring Christianity to native Africans.

In January 1817, African American leaders held a meeting in Allen's Bethel Church. More than three thousand people jammed into the church and milled about outside. After the speakers presented their case for African emigration, they asked for a vote. Three thousand voices shouted "No!" Allen and his friends were stunned.

Few of the people in the crowd had ever seen Africa, and many families had lived in America for generations. They had embraced Christianity and the ideals of democracy. Despite the injustice they suffered, African Americans believed that America was their homeland.

Following this resounding rejection, Allen and his colleagues dropped the plan and published a resolution:

> WHEREAS our ancestors (not of choice) were the first cultivators of the wilds of America, we their descendants feel ourselves entitled to participate in the blessings of her luxuriant soil, which their blood and sweat manured; and that any measure, or system of measures, having a tendency to banish us from her bosom, would not only be cruel, but in direct violation of those principles, which have been the boast of the republick.

MANY PATHS TO EQUALITY

"Those principles, which have been the boast of the republick"—freedom and equality—continued to motivate Allen. His earlier arguments against slavery had been based on religious principles: slavery was a moral evil. Later, he took part in direct political action. During the American Revolution, Patriots had pressured Britain with a boycott of British goods. Now, decades later, abolitionists formed a Free Produce Society of Pennsylvania, refusing to buy any goods made with slave labor. The Colored Free Produce Society, a similar group organized by women in 1831, met in Bethel Church.

Sarah and Richard Allen and other AME members also joined the Underground Railroad. Using their homes as safe havens, members

> ## "HIS HOUSE WAS NEVER SHUT AGAINST THE FRIENDLESS, HOMELESS, PENNILESS FUGITIVES FROM THE 'HOUSE OF BONDAGE.'"
>
> —*Daniel Payne, AME bishop*

hid runaway slaves as they made their way to freedom. The federal Fugitive Slave Law of 1793 didn't protect escaping slaves, even in Pennsylvania, where slavery had been outlawed. Southern owners sent agents north with warrants to arrest runaways.

One of those agents came north with an arrest warrant for Richard Allen, claiming he was a runaway slave. Allen went to jail briefly until the mistake was cleared up. He pressed charges for attempted kidnapping, and the slave catcher spent three months in debtors' prison, unable to pay the bail. Allen knew that other, less prominent African Americans were even more vulnerable to capture and enslavement.

Just as Richard Allen became more than a minister, his church became more than a religious institution. Allen worked to make the African American church a center of social, political, and spiritual life. He used his church pulpit to preach not just religion but social justice. He used public demonstrations and the media to repeat his message.

And Richard Allen preached and practiced nonviolence. More than a century later, when Dr. Martin Luther King, Jr., and others led the campaign for African American civil rights, they could look back to Richard Allen, who had done it all before.

> ## "THIS LAND WHICH WE HAVE WATERED WITH OUR TEARS AND OUR BLOOD IS NOW OUR MOTHER COUNTRY."
>
> —*Richard Allen*

CHAPTER THIRTEEN

JARENA LEE

(1783–1864)

Jarena, a housemaid, took orders from the woman of the house and from the cook. One day, a different voice called to her. "Go preach the Gospel!"

She looked around. "No one will believe me," she replied to the empty room.

The voice spoke again. "Preach the Gospel; I will put words in your mouth, and will turn your enemies to become your friends."

Jarena saw a vision of a church pulpit with a Bible lying on it. Was she seeing and hearing a message from God or the devil? She was a faithful Methodist, a member of Richard Allen's African Methodist Episcopal (AME) Church. She knew about God and the devil.

That night, she dreamed that "there stood before me a great multitude, while I expounded to them the things of religion. So violent were my exertions, and so loud were my exclamations, that I awoke from the sound of my own voice, which also awoke the family of the house where I resided."

The voice, the vision, and the dream convinced Jarena. She would become a preacher. Now she had to convince Richard Allen. Would that famous minister allow a woman, a lowly housemaid, to preach?

Jarena Lee wrote the first African American woman's autobiography, *The Life and Religious Experience of Jarena Lee, a Coloured Lady, Giving an Account of Her Call to Preach the Gospel.* She began with a Bible quote: "And it shall come to pass . . . that I will pour out my Spirit upon all flesh; and your sons, and your *daughters* shall prophecy." Lee put the word *daughters* in italic type to let her readers know where her book and her life were headed.

Jarena was born free in New Jersey on February 11, 1783. The American Revolution had been won and the United States was an independent nation. Northern states were gradually abolishing slavery, and southern slaves were escaping north to freedom. But freedom from slavery didn't mean freedom from poverty.

When she was just seven years old, Jarena was sent sixty miles from home to work as a housemaid. Many black and white families, too poor to feed their children, put them to work at a young age. Jarena didn't write about her childhood—if her employers were kind or cruel, if she had any friends, or if she ever visited her family.

> **"IT WAS THE UNSEEN ARM OF GOD WHICH SAVED ME FROM SELF-MURDER."**
>
> —*Jarena Lee*

When Jarena was twenty-one, she heard a minister preach about the psalm "Lord, I am vile, conceived in sin." The young woman took this to heart. "I was driven of Satan . . . and tempted to destroy myself." She sat on the bank of a stream, thinking that "drowning would be an easy death."

Somehow, she found the strength to resist. She called it "the unseen arm of God." But her feelings of despair didn't go away, and over the next three months she suffered a mental breakdown. Jarena was lucky. The woman she worked for nursed her during this time and "was exceedingly kind."

FINDING HER SPIRITUAL HOME

After Jarena recovered, she moved to Philadelphia and visited several churches, looking for a spiritual home. When she heard Richard Allen preach at the AME Bethel Church, she knew that "this is the people to which my heart unites." She joined Allen's church.

Just three weeks later, she had a profound experience at Bethel. "Though hundreds were present, I did leap to my feet and declare that God, for Christ's sake, had pardoned the sins of my soul." Such "exhortations" were a common practice among Methodists, but only for those who had permission from the minister. Jarena's sudden outburst was most unusual.

In her autobiography, Jarena wrote many pages about her years of doubt and temptation, when she turned again to thoughts of suicide. Richard Allen's powerful sermons were not enough to soothe her soul.

CALLED TO PREACH

When she was twenty-eight, Jarena heard the voice and had the dream about preaching. She felt nervous as she walked to Richard Allen's house to tell the minister about it. So nervous that several times she spun around and headed for home. But each time, she turned back again. The closer Jarena got to Allen's house, the calmer she became.

When she arrived at his door, she felt perfectly calm.

Sitting with the minister, she stated her case simply. "The Lord had revealed it to me, that I must preach the gospel."

A woman preaching. This was something Allen didn't hear every day. Where did she want to preach?

Among the Methodists, and to anyone else who would listen.

Women led prayer meetings in their homes, he told her. But a woman preaching in public? The Methodists did not allow it.

Jarena suddenly felt "that holy energy which burned within me, as a fire, began to be smothered."

"THAT HOLY ENERGY WHICH BURNED WITHIN ME, AS A FIRE, BEGAN TO BE SMOTHERED."

MARRIED TO A MINISTER

Women like Mary Perth had preached to slaves at secret services in the woods. But Richard Allen and other African American men were organizing traditional churches with ministers, church committees, and bishops. What was acceptable in the woods was not allowed in churches. Like white society, African American society was dominated by men with no place in church pulpits for women. Only the Quakers, with no ordained ministers or pulpits, allowed women to preach on equal terms with men.

Soon after Allen's rejection, Jarena married a minister, Joseph Lee, and moved to Snow Hill, an African American village near Philadelphia. She didn't feel at home there, for she "never found that agreement and closeness in communion and fellowship, that I had in Philadelphia." Within a year, she was begging her husband to move back to the city. But he had his church to attend to. She held prayer meetings at home, but it wasn't enough. She sank into a long sickness, and it didn't help that five family members died within a few years, including her husband.

FINDING HER VOICE

Now a widow, Jarena Lee rose from her sickbed, took her two children—James, two years old, and an infant—and returned to Philadelphia. (She doesn't mention the infant again, so it probably didn't survive.) Back among her friends at Bethel Church, Lee once again longed to stand up and be heard.

She went to see Richard Allen, eight years after her first visit. This time he gave her permission to lead prayer meetings and exhort. This meant standing up in church after the minister's sermon to praise his message and to urge others to follow his advice. She wasn't allowed to give messages of her own, though. Lee, with a heart full of passion and plenty to say, could only echo what Richard Allen and other ministers preached.

> **"ONE THING . . . BOUND ME TO EARTH, . . . THAT I HAD NOT AS YET PREACHED THE GOSPEL."**
>
> —*Jarena Lee*

During her prayer meetings, Lee strayed into minister territory, choosing a Bible passage and giving it her own interpretation. Prayers, hymns, and Bible messages made her prayer meetings like church services. "Some wept, while others shouted for joy. One whole seat of females, by the power of God . . . were all bowed to the floor, at once, and screamed out." Such emotional outbursts had become common in African American churches.

Stories about Jarena Lee traveled beyond Philadelphia, and she went to preach thirty miles away, leaving her young son with Sarah

ANSWERING THE CRY FOR FREEDOM

Allen, Richard's wife. Lee's first trip lasted a week, and she was so focused on her preaching that "not a thought of my little son came into my mind."

Encouraged by her preaching success, Lee gave up her home in Philadelphia and left her son with the Allens. Richard Allen gave her a license as a traveling preacher of the AME Church, but she could not become an official minister. Allen was bending the rules even by allowing her to preach.

ON THE ROAD

Jarena Lee, an uneducated housemaid, had the courage to challenge male authority and make her way through a country riddled with racism and sexism. She spent thirty years traveling and preaching. She kept a detailed journal, recording how far she traveled and where she went. She preached to Methodists and Baptists, Quakers, Presbyterians, and Episcopalians. She preached to slave owners, slaves, and Native Americans. She preached in white churches, black churches, and integrated churches; in schoolhouses, courthouses, private homes and barns, and at outdoor camp meetings.

> **"BY THE INSTRUMENTALITY [ACTIONS] OF A POOR COLOURED WOMAN, THE LORD POURED FORTH HIS SPIRIT AMONG THE PEOPLE."**
>
> —*Jarena Lee*

She nursed the sick, buried the dead, and even taught school for a while. She encountered many kindnesses and conflicts. One old man, a cruel slave owner, argued that "he did not believe the coloured people had any souls—he was sure they had none." Yet her sermon that day convinced him he was wrong and she wrote, "he became greatly altered in his ways for the better."

She met with more opposition to her gender than to her race. Both white and black churchmen gave her trouble for being a preaching woman. But if a church was locked against her, people offered their homes. If no home was near, she preached outdoors. To one hostile minister she said, "If an ass reproved Balaam . . . why should not a woman reprove sin? . . . May be a speaking woman is like an ass—but I can tell you one thing, the ass saw the angel when Balaam didn't." Jarena knew her Bible stories and used them to make her point.

"GLORY TO GOD'S DEAR NAME, WE HAD A MOST MELTING, SIN-KILLING, AND SOUL-REVIVING TIME."

—*Jarena Lee*

She returned to Philadelphia many times, staying for a few days, weeks, or months with her son, James. One day, when he was five, he stood up on a chair and belted out a hymn. His proud mother fell to her knees and sang along, certain that the boy's soul was saved. James lived with Richard and Sarah Allen and went to school until he was a teenager. Then Lee found him an apprenticeship with a cabinetmaker. Though she was not a traditional mother, she saw to it that her son grew up in a loving home and acquired a skilled trade.

Richard Allen continued to be Lee's steadfast champion. He invited her to preach at Bethel Church when she was in Philadelphia, despite complaints from other ministers. Allen and Lee attended several conventions of Methodist leaders in Baltimore, and he asked her to preach with him. After Allen died in 1831, she lost those privileges.

"I WAS TEMPTED TO WITHDRAW FROM THE METHODIST CHURCH."

Bethel ministers grudgingly allowed Lee to preach, but only on Thursday nights. Allen had let her preach any day, any time. At one point, she wrote: "The oppositions I met with . . . were numerous—so much so, that I was tempted to withdraw from the Methodist Church." A woman friend listened to her woes, urged her to go on; "I embraced the sister in my arms, and we had a melting time together."

FULFILLING HER DREAM

Jarena Lee didn't like lingering anywhere, even in Philadelphia. "My mind soon became oppressed and craved to travel." Through the years, she traveled thousands of miles, usually on her own, something

"MY MIND . . . CRAVED TO TRAVEL."

most women didn't do. She walked; she rode in carts and stagecoaches on unpaved roads, on new railroads, and on riverboats, where she got dreadfully seasick.

She traveled to Snow Hill and preached in the church where her husband had been the minister. "The thought made me tremble," but she did it. On she went, into Maryland and Delaware, both slave states, through Pennsylvania and New York State along the Erie Canal to Ohio and Canada.

In Canada, Lee met many former American slaves who had escaped there to freedom. She said, "This was the first time I ever breathed pure air." She urged the new Canadians to build schools for their children and hire white teachers. She insisted that "without the advantages of education they never would be a moral people, and, in the course of time, their own children could, by proper advancement, become teachers for themselves." Inspired by Lee, several black churches established schools for their children.

Back in the United States, Jarena Lee didn't just preach religion. She joined the American Antislavery Society and spoke out for abolition. Like her mentor, Richard Allen, she linked her religious faith to racial politics. Of those who defended slavery, she wrote: "The wickedness of the people certainly calls for the lowering Judgments of God to be let loose upon the Nation and Slavery, that wretched system that eminated from the bottomless pit, is one of the greatest curses to any Nation."

> "I HAD BUT THREE OR FOUR CENTS IN MY POCKET.... AFTER I HAD SPOKEN, THEIR CONTRIBUTION FOR ME AMOUNTED TO FOUR OR FIVE DOLLARS; WHICH AIDED ME ON MY JOURNEY."
>
> —*Jarena Lee*

> "SLAVERY, THAT WRETCHED SYSTEM THAT EMINATED FROM THE BOTTOMLESS PIT, IS ONE OF THE GREATEST CURSES TO ANY NATION."

Though she had no fixed home and relied on the charity of strangers, Lee lived the life she wanted. She enjoyed preaching to pious Christians, but she felt satisfied only when people "fell to the floor under the influence of God's power" during her sermons. When such dramatic events didn't happen, Lee thought "it was a dull time indeed." After addressing a group of Native Americans, she wrote: "We might call them heathens, but they are endowed with a Christian spirit." When she described slaves who walked twenty, thirty, even seventy miles to hear her preach, "my heart glows with joy while I write."

In Ohio, Lee met a Presbyterian woman, "very rich as regards this world's goods," who wanted to preach, but her church and her husband stopped her. She had "a broken heart and a contrite spirit." Another woman who spoke out "for the cause of God" when she taught Sunday school suffered "much opposition, even from her husband; although he was a Preacher of the Gospel."

Lee, free of husband, churchmen, and worldly goods, felt fortunate indeed. Several times during her early life, Lee suffered from depression and even considered suicide. Once she set out into the world to preach, she suffered some disappointments and ill health, but she wrote no more of depression and despair.

"GLORY TO GOD FOR WHAT MY HEART FEELS WHILE I USE MY PEN IN HAND."

—*Jarena Lee*

WRITING HER STORY

In her fifties, Lee wrote her autobiography. With only three months of formal schooling, she paid a writer $5 to "corrected it for press." In 1836, she paid $38 to have one thousand copies printed. When she sold them all, she had another thousand copies printed.

> **"I COMMENCED TRAVELLING AGAIN, FEELING IT BETTER TO WEAR OUT THAN TO RUST OUT."**

She asked her church's book committee to help pay for an expanded version of the autobiography, but the committee refused. It wasn't a good book, the members said. "It is impossible to decipher much of the meaning contained in it." Traveling preachers weren't allowed to publish books without official approval, but Lee ignored the rules. In 1849, she paid to print the expanded version of the book.

Though Lee was a serious woman and deplored "carnal amusements," such as dancing, she showed a sense of humor at the end of her book: "I commenced travelling again, feeling it better to wear out than to rust out." At age sixty-six, she took to the road again.

A CHAMPION FOR WOMEN

Jarena Lee rejected the traditional woman's roles of keeping house and raising children. She was full of spiritual and political fire and she challenged the male power structure. Richard Allen gave her certain liberties to preach, but she took even more: she wrote and published her life story, not once but twice. Allen's Bethel Church strove to bring justice to African Americans. Jarena Lee expanded that goal to include equal opportunity for women.

In 1850, a committee of traveling female preachers applied to become licensed ministers in the AME Church. If

> **"WHY SHOULD IT BE THOUGHT IMPOSSIBLE . . . OR IMPROPER FOR A WOMAN TO PREACH? SEEING THE SAVIOUR DIED FOR THE WOMAN AS WELL AS FOR THE MAN."**

Jarena Lee had been in town, she certainly would have endorsed that proposal. The women submitted their request to the AME churchmen and it was roundly rejected.

For decades, Jarena Lee argued fiercely for equality for women in the church, by her words and her deeds. She did not want her own, or any woman's, "holy energy" smothered by male authority. She demanded, "Why should it be thought impossible . . . or improper for a woman to preach? seeing the Saviour died for the woman as well as for the man." If the gift of preaching is given by God, would he only choose to give the gift to men? She replied, "As for me, I am fully persuaded that the Lord called me to labor according to what I received, in his vineyard."

ECHOES OF THE CRY FOR FREEDOM

After the American Revolution was won, the Founding Fathers wrote a constitution to protect individual human rights. But a ferocious debate arose about a glaring contradiction to those rights: slavery. The Founding Fathers realized that a union of thirteen very different states was a fragile one and that the issue of slavery could break it apart. To preserve national unity, they allowed each state to determine policies about slavery. Northern states began to abolish it, while slavery expanded southward and westward.

The enslaved population nearly tripled between 1770 and 1810: from 470,000 to 1,200,000. As slavery declined in the north, the free African American population grew. It more than tripled after the war, from 60,000 in 1790 to 185,000 in 1810. But free blacks were not equal to white Americans, and states began to pass laws to make sure that situation continued. Special taxes were levied on free blacks, they were denied the vote in some states, and Ohio tried to prevent them from settling there.

MANY ROADS TO FREEDOM

Despite southern slavery and northern inequality, the American Revolution did have important positive consequences for African Americans. They had listened as white Americans discussed the right to life and liberty, and blacks believed it applied to them. They watched white Patriots plan political protests, and they began to organize and speak for themselves. In 1773, Phillis Wheatley spoke in poetry:

> *I, young in life, by seeming cruel fate*
> *Was snatch'd from Afric's fancy'd happy seat:*
> . . . .
> *Such, such my case. And can I then but pray*
> *Others may never feel tyrannic sway?*

Prince Hall founded the first African Masonic Lodge, a well-respected platform to campaign for African American rights. Richard Allen founded a church, and Jarena Lee defied that church to claim the freedom to preach. Paul Cuffe and colleagues used the Patriots' slogan "no taxation without representation" and refused to pay taxes because African Americans couldn't vote. Elizabeth "Mumbet" Freeman sued for her freedom in a court of law and won.

James Armistead Lafayette petitioned the Virginia legislature twice for his freedom after serving in the Continental army. Ona Judge, Boston King, John Kizell, and Mary Perth protested with their feet and ran away from slavery. Agrippa Hull sheltered runaway slaves, and Sally Hemings bargained for her children's freedom. African Americans staged many sorts of nonviolent actions to gain their rights.

INDEPENDENT SPIRITS

Richard Allen founded the African Methodist Episcopal (AME) Church, which became a powerful spiritual and political center for African Americans. When Paul Cuffe traveled to Sierra Leone, he saw former slaves like Mary Perth, Boston King, and John Kizell using their churches to educate their children and petition for political rights. The ideals of the American Revolution had crossed an ocean.

Many in white society deplored such spirited independence among African Americans. A white Methodist in 1830 complained, "Their aspirings and little vanities have been rapidly growing since they got those separate churches. . . . Thirty to forty years ago, they were much humbler, more esteemed in their places, and more useful to themselves and others."

An African American bishop later defined these "aspirings and little vanities" in this way: "They dared to organize a Church of men, men to think for themselves, men to talk for themselves, men to act for themselves." Jarena Lee displayed the same spirited independence.

The struggle to end slavery and gain equality would be long and difficult. But African Americans claimed the legacy of the American Revolution for themselves and for their children. And that meant equal rights and opportunities in a free, democratic, and multiracial society.

AUTHOR NOTES AND TIMELINES

BOSTON KING

The Black Loyalist Heritage Society and Old School House Museum in Birchtown, Nova Scotia, Canada, celebrate the lives of Boston King and his fellow settlers (blackloyalist.com). *The Life of Boston King*, published by the Nova Scotia Museum and Nimbus Publishing, includes King's autobiography along with essays about him and his family.

CA. 1760 Born enslaved on Richard Waring's plantation near Charleston, South Carolina.

1776 Apprenticed to a carpenter in Charleston.

1780 British capture Charleston; King escapes to freedom and joins British army.

1782 Americans recapture Charleston; King retreats with British to New York City.

1783 King and his wife, Violet, emigrate to Nova Scotia with Black Loyalists.

1791 Appointed Methodist preacher.

1792 Sails to Sierra Leone; Violet dies.

1793 Appointed Methodist teacher and missionary to Africans.

1794–96 Sails to England; studies at Kingswood School; writes autobiography.

1796–1802 Returns to Sierra Leone; teaches among native Africans.

1802 Dies in Sierra Leone.

AGRIPPA HULL

In 1844, when he was eighty-five, Agrippa Hull paid $3 to have his photograph taken. Sometime after that, an artist painted Hull's portrait from the photograph. The painting now hangs in the library of Hull's hometown, Stockbridge, Massachusetts (pbs.org/wgbh/aia/part2/2h.8).

1759 MARCH 7—Born free in Northampton, Massachusetts.

1777 Joins Continental army; assigned as orderly to General John Paterson; Battle of Saratoga begins.

1777–78 Endures winter with army at Valley Forge, Pennsylvania.

1779 Assigned as an orderly to Colonel Tadeuz Kościuszko, military engineer.

1780–83 Fights in North and South Carolina with Kościuszko and Continental army.

1783 Peace treaty signed. Hull discharged from army; returns to Stockbridge, Massachusetts; begins work for twenty years as servant to Theodore Sedgwick, lawyer and politician.

1785 Buys first piece of land in Stockbridge and gradually increases landholdings; marries Jane Darby and they eventually have four children. Jane's date of death is unknown.

1797 Travels to New York City to see Kościuszko, who is touring the United States.

1822 Marries Margaret (Peggy) Timbroke; the couple work as caterers.

1828 Receives veteran's pension.

1831 Visits West Point, New York, with Stockbridge citizens to view statue of Kościuszko.

1848 MAY 21—Dies in Stockbridge, Massachusetts.

JAMES ARMISTEAD LAFAYETTE

A portrait of James Armistead Lafayette, painted by John Blennerhassett Martin in 1824, is on display at the Valentine Museum in Richmond, Virginia (thevalentine.org/blog/RVAS-james-armistead-lafayette).

CA. 1748 Born enslaved in Virginia.

1781 MARCH—Joins Marquis de Lafayette's Continental army troops at Yorktown; works as a "pioneer."

1781 SPRING—British general Cornwallis arrives in Yorktown. James crosses British lines, becomes Cornwallis's waiter, and spies for Lafayette.

SUMMER—Ordered by Cornwallis to spy on Americans; becomes double agent.

AUTUMN—Siege of Yorktown; Cornwallis and British army surrender. James is revealed as a loyal American; returns to slavery.

1784 Petitions Virginia legislature for freedom; petition is ignored.

1786 Petitions legislature again.

1787 Granted freedom and forty acres of land; chooses a new name: James Armistead Lafayette.

1818 Applies for soldier's pension; granted $40 a year.

1824 Lafayette returns to the United States; greets James in Richmond; James's portrait is painted.

1830 Dies in Virginia.

PHILLIS WHEATLEY

A copy of Phillis Wheatley's *Poems on Various Subjects, Religious and Moral* with Scipio Moorhead's portrait is held at the Massachusetts Historical Society in Boston (masshist.org/database/52).

In a corner of the Society stands Phillis Wheatley's writing desk. She carried this mahogany table from the Wheatley home, to the places she lived with John Peters, and to the boardinghouse where she died. After Wheatley's death, the table was bought by a relative of Revolutionary War general Israel Putnam. It remained in the family for nearly two hundred years, passing from mother to eldest daughter. In 1992, the desk was donated to the Massachusetts Historical Society (masshist.org/database/363).

In November 2005, a letter from Phillis Wheatley to Obour Tanner, dated February 14, 1776, sold for $253,000 to a private collector.

CA. 1753 Born free in Africa.

1761 Enslaved and transported to Boston; bought by John and Susanna Wheatley.

1767 First poem printed in Newport, Rhode Island, newspaper.

1772 Interviewed by Boston elite to prove her authorship of poems.

1773 Travels to England; celebrated by nobility. Phillis's book of poems is published in London. She returns to Boston; freed by John Wheatley.

1774 Susanna Wheatley dies.

1776 Writes poem for George Washington; meets him in Cambridge, Massachusetts.

1778 John Wheatley dies; Phillis marries John Peters.

1779 Attempts to publish second book of poems and is unsuccessful.

1784 DECEMBER 5—Dies in Boston.

ELIZABETH "MUMBET" FREEMAN

A small portrait of Elizabeth "Mumbet" Freeman was painted by Susan Ridley Sedgwick in 1811, when Mumbet was nearly seventy. It is owned by the Massachusetts Historical Society (masshist.org/gallery/item?item=23).

The Ashley House in Sheffield, Massachusetts, Freeman's home when she was enslaved, is open to visitors during the summer. A few decades ago, tour guides at the house focused on Colonel John Ashley. Today, visitors hear much more about Elizabeth Freeman—Mumbet—the slave who stood up to the most powerful man in town (thetrustees.org/places-to-visit/berkshires/ashley-house).

CA. 1742 Born enslaved in New York State; given to Hannah Ashley upon her marriage to John Ashley, date unknown; taken to Sheffield, Massachusetts.

1780 Constitution of the Commonwealth of Massachusetts declares "All men are born free and equal."

1781 Files lawsuit for freedom; freed in jury trial; chooses name: Elizabeth Freeman.

1781–1808 Works as a housekeeper for Theodore Sedgwick in Stockbridge; serves as village midwife.

1787 Defends Sedgwick home against Shays' Rebellion rebels.

1807 Purchases parcel of land in Stockbridge; adds to her land in 1809, 1811; retires from Sedgwick household; lives with her family on her land.

1829 DECEMBER 28—Dies in Stockbridge, Massachusetts.

PRINCE HALL

Prince Hall is buried in Copp's Hill Burying Ground in Boston, where his modest gravestone is timeworn and broken. In 1835, a much grander monument was placed next to his grave by the Most Worshipful Prince Hall Grand Lodge of Massachusetts.

CA. 1735 Born enslaved, birthplace unknown.

1749 Bought by William Hall, Boston leatherworker.

1756 Marries Delia, a slave; son Primus born; Delia dies, date unknown.

1763 Marries Sarah Richie, a slave. She dies before 1770.

1768–75 British army occupies Boston to quell revolutionary activity.

1770 Freed by William Hall; sets up leather business; marries Flora Gibbs.

1775 Applies to the Masonic Lodge in Boston for membership and is rejected; accepted by British Masons; forms African Lodge No. 1; chosen as Grand Master.

1777 Sends petition to state legislature to abolish slavery; petition is ignored.

1784 Applies to Boston Masons for permanent charter and is refused; receives British charter; son Africanus born.

1787 Petitions Boston selectmen for schools for black children; petition is ignored.

1788 Works to recover three kidnapped free blacks.

1796 Sends another petition for black schools; petition is ignored.

1798 Marries Sylvia Ward; son Primus opens school in his home.

1807 Dies in Boston.

1808 African Masonic Lodges renamed Prince Hall Lodges.

MARY PERTH

American historians have paid little attention to Mary Perth, a Black Loyalist. It took an Australian, Dr. Cassandra Pybus, to unearth her story.

CA. 1740 Born, birthplace unknown.

1767 Recorded in John Willoughby's tax report in Virginia.

1775 Willoughby is arrested as a Loyalist; his slaves are ordered seized.

1776 Mary, her three children, and all of Willoughby's slaves escape to the British army; gain freedom as Black Loyalists; Mary and children survive smallpox and typhoid epidemics; sail to New York City.

CA. 1780 Marries Caesar Perth.

1783 American Revolution ends; family settles in Nova Scotia; daughter Susan born.

1792 Family sails to Freetown, Sierra Leone; Caesar dies.

1792–1801 Owns a shop; works as a housekeeper to the English governor and a housemother for schoolboys.

1794 Escapes with schoolboys to nearby village during French navy attack.

1799–1801 Travels to England to care for schoolboys; Susan dies.

1801 Returns to Sierra Leone.

1806 Remarries.

1813 Dies in Freetown, Sierra Leone.

ONA JUDGE

The ad announcing Ona Judge's escape, placed in the *Philadelphia Gazette and Daily Advertiser* on May 24, 1796, was discovered by historians only in 2009 (mountvernon.org/research-collections/digital-encyclopedia/article/oney-judge).

1773 Born enslaved in Mount Vernon, Virginia; owned by Martha Washington.

1789 George Washington travels north to take office as first U.S. president; Judge travels as Martha Washington's maid.

1793 George Washington signs Fugitive Slave Law to return runaway slaves to owners.

1796 MAY—Escapes from the Washingtons.

 SUMMER—Sails to Portsmouth, New Hampshire.

 SEPTEMBER—Washington tries to have Judge kidnapped; his plan fails.

 NOVEMBER—Washington tries again to have Judge seized and fails again.

1797 JANUARY—Marries Jack Staines, a free black seaman.

1798–1803 Children Eliza, Nancy, and William are born.

1799 AUTUMN—Martha Washington's nephew comes for Judge; she escapes.

1803 Husband dies.

1803–48 Lives with friends; works as a housemaid.

1820s Son William lost at sea.

1830s Daughters Eliza and Nancy die.

1840s Judge and friends listed as paupers and are supported by the town.

1846 Gives two interviews to newspapers.

1848 Dies in Greenland, New Hampshire.

SALLY HEMINGS

For nearly two hundred years, the claim that Thomas Jefferson had fathered children with a slave named Sally was denied by scholars as "unworthy" of the great man. Jefferson's white family rejected the rumors as well. However, there is no credible evidence proving that someone else fathered Sally's children, and the evidence for Jefferson's paternity is substantial:

- DNA testing in 1998 linked the Jefferson family to the descendants of Eston Hemings, Sally's son.
- Jefferson was present at Monticello nine months before each birth.
- No written accounts claimed that Sally ever had a relationship with any other man.

Historians at the Thomas Jefferson Foundation at Monticello accept that he is the most probable father of Sally Hemings's children. Though some white descendants of Jefferson's refuse to accept this evidence, other Jefferson family members hold reunions with their Hemings relatives.

1773 Born enslaved in Virginia, half sister to Thomas Jefferson's wife, Martha.

1774 Moves to Monticello, Jefferson's home, with mother and siblings.

1784 Jefferson moves to Paris as U.S. ambassador.

1787 Accompanies Jefferson's younger daughter to Paris as her maid.

1789 Becomes pregnant with Jefferson's child; returns to Virginia.

1789–1808 Gives birth to six children; three sons and one daughter survive; remains at Monticello when Jefferson serves as vice president and president.

1809–26 Works as Jefferson's personal servant when he retires to Monticello.

1822 Son Beverly and daughter, Harriet, leave for Washington, D.C.; "pass" into white world.

1826 Jefferson dies; frees five of his 130 slaves at Monticello, including sons Madison and Eston Hemings. Sally Hemings is unofficially freed; moves to Charlottesville, Virginia, with her two sons.

1835 Dies in Charlottesville.

PAUL CUFFE

A silhouette of Paul Cuffe, painted during his visit to England, is on display at the New Bedford Whaling Museum in Massachusetts (whalingmuseum.org).

1759 Born free in Cuttyhunk, Massachusetts.

1773 Goes to sea as a common hand.

1775 Captured by British navy; held prisoner for three months.

1780 Refuses to pay taxes without the right to vote.

1780 ONWARD—Begins shipbuilding and trading business; captains his ships with multiracial crews.

1783 Massachusetts legislature grants African American men their voting rights. Marries Alice Pequit; they eventually have seven children.

1797 Proposes town school but citizens reject proposal; builds Cuff's School.

1810 Sails to Africa to create a trading network with the United States.

1811 Sails to England to promote African trade.

1812 Returns to the United States; Cuffe's cargo is impounded; appeals to the president for its return.

1815 Returns to Africa, this time with thirty-eight African American settlers.

1816 Exposes illegal American slave traders.

1817 Dies in Westport, Massachusetts.

JOHN KIZELL

The remarkable story of John Kizell remained buried in British and American archives until Kevin G. Lowther, an American historian, published Kizell's biography in 2011.

CA. 1760 Born free in West Africa.

1773 Captured, enslaved, and transported to South Carolina; bought by Charleston innkeeper.

1780 Escapes to freedom when British army captures Charleston; joins British army.

1782 Escapes to New York City when British army retreats from Charleston.

1783 Sails with wife, Phillis, to Nova Scotia, Canada.

1792 Sails to Sierra Leone with Black Loyalists.

1790s–1800s Establishes a prosperous trading business; becomes Baptist preacher.

1810 Works with English governor in Sierra Leone to convince Africans to quit trading in slaves, without success.

1820 Welcomes eighty-four African American settlers to Sherbro Island.

1825 Appointed superintendent of twenty thousand Africans liberated from slave ships.

1830 Last record of Kizell; date and place of his death unknown.

RICHARD ALLEN

Allen dictated an account of his life—*The Life, Experience, and Gospel Labours of the Rt. Rev. Richard Allen. To Which Is Annexed the Rise and Progress of the African Methodist Episcopal Church in the United States of America*—to his son near the end of his life. Today, the African Methodist Episcopal (AME) Church has over seven thousand churches in thirty countries around the world, with more than two million members.

1760 FEBRUARY 14—Born enslaved in Philadelphia.

1767 Sold with his family to Stokeley Sturgis of Delaware.

1777 Converts to Methodism.

1780–83 Signs contract with Sturgis to buy his freedom; travels the countryside working and preaching.

1783 Makes his final payment for freedom; chooses the name Richard Allen.

1783–86 Works as a traveling peddler and preacher.

1786 Moves to Philadelphia; attends white Methodist church.

1790 Marries Flora.

1792 Stages walkout at white Methodist church.

1793 Yellow-fever epidemic erupts. Allen helps with relief work; publishes rebuttal of Mathew Carey's criticism; includes antislavery tract.

1794 Opens first Bethel AME Church; chosen as minister.

1794–1816 Files lawsuit against white Methodists over control of AME Church; church finally declared independent.

1797–1831 Allen's home and church serve as a stop on the Underground Railroad.

1799 Writes eulogy for George Washington.

1801 Wife Flora dies childless. Allen marries Sarah; they eventually have six children.

1815 Supports African American resettlement in Africa.

1816 Elected first AME bishop.

1817 Church members reject Allen's plan for resettlement in Africa.

1831 MARCH 26—Dies in Philadelphia.

1833 Autobiography published.

JARENA LEE

A portrait of Jarena Lee, at age sixty, was published in the 1849 edition of her autobiography, *The Life and Religious Experience of Jarena Lee, a Coloured Lady.* Lee's legacy today includes the Jarena Lee Professorship of Pastoral Care and Counseling at the Interdenominational Theological Center in Atlanta, Georgia; and the Jarena Lee Preaching Academy in Northampton, Massachusetts, which offers workshops for African American women (blackpast.org/aah/lee-jarena-1783).

1783 FEBRUARY 11—Born free in Cape May, New Jersey.

1790 Sent to work as a servant.

1804 Considers suicide; experiences a mental collapse.

1805 Moves to Philadelphia; joins Bethel AME Church.

1811 Hears voices to preach, but AME minister Richard Allen forbids it; marries Methodist minister Joseph Lee and moves to a village near Philadelphia.

1816 Lee's husband dies. Lee returns to Philadelphia with young son.

1819 Receives license from Allen to become a traveling preacher.

1820s–ON Leaves son with the Allens and travels thousands of miles preaching, against much opposition from men.

CA. 1833 Begins writing her autobiography.

1836 Pays $38 for printing one thousand copies of her autobiography.

1849 Pays to print an expanded version of her book.

1864 FEBRUARY 5—Dies in Philadelphia.

ACKNOWLEDGMENTS

During my research for one book, I often find the subject for my next one. And so it was with *Answering the Cry for Freedom*. Working on a book about Elizabeth "Mumbet" Freeman led me to other African Americans who lived during the American Revolution. As I learned more (and more) about them, I wanted to write not single biographies but a collage of lives, offering a wider perspective to an era that usually focuses on white males. My research files grew and grew until I trimmed my subjects to an even dozen. Then I discovered Jarena Lee, and I couldn't leave her out. So I've written about the lives of thirteen remarkable people.

Six years of work went into *Answering the Cry for Freedom*, and many people helped by locating materials, answering questions, and critiquing the manuscript. Gary B. Nash, distinguished research professor, UCLA, met with me at the beginning of my research and read the final manuscript. Mary Thompson, research historian at Mount Vernon, provided important information along the way, including the newly discovered ad for "ABSCONDED" Ona Judge. Historian Barbara Dowling proved a most instructive tour guide of Sheffield and Stockbridge, Massachusetts.

I encountered many other helpful kindred souls during my travels from Monticello in Virginia to the Black Loyalist Heritage Society in Shelburne, Nova Scotia. They helped me "find" my subjects in their home territories and added local knowledge and color to the stories of Sally Hemings (Monticello), Ona Judge (Mount Vernon, Virginia, and Portsmouth Historical Society, New Hampshire), Richard Allen and Jarena Lee (AME Bethel Church, Philadelphia), Elizabeth "Mumbet" Freeman and Agrippa Hull (Sheffield and Stockbridge, Massachusetts), Prince Hall and Phillis Wheatley (Massachusetts Historical Society and Museum of African American History, Boston), Paul Cuffe (New Bedford Whaling Museum, Massachusetts), and Boston King, Mary Perth, and John Kizell (Black Loyalist Heritage Society).

My venerable critique group—Caroline Arnold, Nina Kidd, Alexis O'Neill, and Ann Redisch Stampler—read many versions of many chapters through the years and offered cogent suggestions and constant encouragement. My editor and friend Carolyn P. Yoder added her historical and literary prowess to the last drafts. She also brought R. Gregory Christie to the project, and I'm thrilled to see his artwork enhance these people's stories.

Thank you to everyone.

Mirroring the esteem I hold for the men and women in *Answering the Cry for Freedom* is the deep admiration I feel for the many young people working for social and environmental justice in our time. And so I dedicate this book to them, especially my son and daughter, Cleo and Alice Woelfle-Erskine.

—GW

SELECTED BIBLIOGRAPHY*

REVOLUTIONARY WAR HISTORY

Aptheker, Herbert. *The Negro in the American Revolution*. New York: International Publishers, 1940.

Bennett, Lerone, Jr. *Pioneers in Protest*. Chicago: Johnson Publishing, 1968.

Berlin, Ira. *Many Thousands Gone: The First Two Centuries of Slavery in North America*. Cambridge, MA: Belknap Press of Harvard University Press, 1998.

Foner, Philip S. *Blacks in the American Revolution*. Westport, CT: Greenwood Press, 1976.

Frey, Sylvia R. *Water from the Rock: Black Resistance in a Revolutionary Age*. Princeton, NJ: Princeton University Press, 1991.

Gottschalk, Louis, ed. *The Letters of Lafayette to Washington, 1777–1799*. New York: H. F. Hubbard, 1944.

Jordan, Winthrop D. *The White Man's Burden: Historical Origins of Racism in the United States*. New York: Oxford University Press, 1974.

———. *White over Black: American Attitudes Toward the Negro, 1550–1812*. Chapel Hill: University of North Carolina Press, 1968.

Kaplan, Sidney, and Emma Nogrady Kaplan. *The Black Presence in the Era of the American Revolution*. Rev. ed. Amherst: University of Massachusetts Press, 1989.

Martin, James Kirby, ed. *Ordinary Courage: The Revolutionary War Adventures of Joseph Plumb Martin*. St. James, NY: Brandywine Press, 1993.

McManus, Edgar J. *Black Bondage in the North*. Syracuse, NY: Syracuse University Press, 1973.

Nash, Gary B. *Forging Freedom: The Formation of Philadelphia's Black Community, 1720–1840*. Cambridge, MA: Harvard University Press, 1988.

———. *The Forgotten Fifth: African Americans in the Age of Revolution*. Cambridge, MA: Harvard University Press, 2006.

———. *Race and Revolution*. Madison, WI: Madison House, 1990.

———. *The Unknown American Revolution: The Unruly Birth of Democracy and the Struggle to Create America*. New York: Viking, 2005.

Pybus, Cassandra. *Epic Journeys of Freedom: Runaway Slaves of the American Revolution and Their Global Quest for Liberty*. Boston: Beacon Press, 2006.

Quarles, Benjamin. *The Negro in the American Revolution*. Chapel Hill: University of North Carolina Press, 1961.

———. *The Negro in the Making of America*. New York: Collier Books, 1987.

Schama, Simon. *Rough Crossings: Britain, the Slaves, and the American Revolution*. New York: Ecco/HarperCollins, 2006.

*Websites active at time of publication

Sidbury, James. *Becoming African in America: Race and Nation in the Early Black Atlantic.* New York: Oxford University Press, 2007.

Walker, James W. St. G. *The Black Loyalists: The Search for a Promised Land in Nova Scotia and Sierra Leone, 1783–1870.* New York: Africana Publishing, 1976.

Wilson, Ellen Gibson. *The Loyal Blacks.* New York: Capricorn Books, 1976.

Young, Alfred F., Gary B. Nash, and Ray Raphael, eds. *Revolutionary Founders: Rebels, Radicals, and Reformers in the Making of the Nation.* New York: Knopf, 2011.

RICHARD ALLEN

Allen, Richard. *The Life, Experience, and Gospel Labours of the Rt. Rev. Richard Allen.* Philadelphia: Martin and Boden, Printers, 1833. docsouth.unc.edu/neh/allen/allen.html.

Nash, Gary B. "New Light on Richard Allen: The Early Years of Freedom." *William and Mary Quarterly,* 3rd ser., 46, no. 2 (April 1989): 332–40.

Newman, Richard S. *Freedom's Prophet: Bishop Richard Allen, the AME Church, and the Black Founding Fathers.* New York: New York University Press, 2008.

———. "Prince Hall, Richard Allen, and Daniel Coker: Revolutionary Black Founders, Revolutionary Black Communities." In *Revolutionary Founders: Rebels, Radicals, and Reformers in the Making of the Nation,* edited by Alfred F. Young, Gary B. Nash, and Ray Raphael, pp. 310–16.

PAUL CUFFE

Delaware Society for the Abolition of Slavery. "Memoirs of the Life of Paul Cuffee, the Interesting Negro Navigator." *Belfast Monthly Magazine* 7, no. 39 (October 31, 1811): 284–92. jstor.org/stable/30074388.

Kaplan, Sidney, and Emma Nogrady Kaplan. *The Black Presence in the Era of the American Revolution,* pp. 151–64.

Senneh, Lamin. *Abolitionists Abroad: American Blacks and the Making of Modern West Africa.* Cambridge, MA: Harvard University Press, 2000, pp. 88–98.

Sidbury, James. *Becoming African in America: Race and Nation in the Early Black Atlantic,* pp. 131–55.

Thomas, Lamont D. *Rise to Be a People: A Biography of Paul Cuffe.* Urbana: University of Illinois Press, 1986.

Wiggins, Rosalind Cobb, ed. *Captain Paul Cuffe's Logs and Letters, 1808–1817.* Washington, DC: Howard University Press, 1996.

ELIZABETH "MUMBET" FREEMAN

Piper, Emilie, and David Levinson. *One Minute a Free Woman: Elizabeth Freeman and the Struggle for Freedom.* Salisbury, CT: Upper Housatonic Valley National Heritage Area, 2010.

Preiss, Lillian E. *Sheffield: Frontier Town.* Sheffield, MA: Sheffield Bicentennial Committee, 1976.

Sedgwick, Catharine Maria. *The Power of Her Sympathy: The Autobiography and Journal of Catharine Maria Sedgwick.* Edited by Mary Kelley. Boston: Massachusetts Historical Society, 1993.

———. "Slavery in New England." *Bentley's Miscellany*, vol. 34 (October 1853): 417–24. play.google.com/books/reader?id=8-ARAAAAYAAJ&printsec=frontcover&output=reader&hl=en&pg=GBS.PA417.

Welch, Richard E., Jr. "Mumbet and Judge Sedgwick." *Boston Bar Journal* 8, no. 1 (Jan. 1964): 12–18.

Zilversmit, Arthur. "Mumbet: Folklore and Fact." *Berkshire History* 1, no. 1 (Spring 1971): 2–14.

———. "Quok Walker, Mumbet, and the Abolition of Slavery in Massachusetts." *William and Mary Quarterly*, 3rd ser., 25, no. 4 (October): 614–24.

PRINCE HALL

African Americans and the End of Slavery in Massachusetts. "St. George Tucker's Queries on Slavery in Massachusetts." Belknap Papers, Massachusetts Historical Society. masshist.org/endofslavery/index.php?id=52.

Hall, Prince, et al. "Petition for freedom (manuscript copy) to the Massachusetts Council and the House of Representatives [13] January 1777." Belknap Papers, Massachusetts Historical Society. masshist.org/database/557.

———. "Petition of Prince Hall to the Massachusetts General Court, 27 February 1788." Belknap Papers, Massachusetts Historical Society. masshist.org/database/670.

Haywood, Charles F. "The Turtle Feast." In *Minutemen and Mariners: True Tales of New England*, pp. 166–76. New York: Dodd Mead, 1963.

Kaplan, Sidney, and Emma Nogrady Kaplan. *The Black Presence in the Era of the American Revolution*, pp. 202–14.

Newman, Richard S. "Prince Hall, Richard Allen, and Daniel Coker: Revolutionary Black Founders, Revolutionary Black Communities." In *Revolutionary Founders: Rebels, Radicals, and Reformers in the Making of the Nation*, edited by Alfred F. Young, Gary B. Nash, and Ray Raphael, pp. 305–10.

Wesley, Charles H. *Prince Hall: Life and Legacy.* Washington, DC: United Supreme Council, Southern Jurisdiction, Prince Hall Affiliation, 1977.

SALLY HEMINGS

Bacon, Edmund. "Mr. Jefferson's Servants." Frontline. pbs.org/wgbh/pages/frontline/shows/jefferson/slaves/bacon.html.

Brodie, Fawn M. *Thomas Jefferson: An Intimate History.* New York: Norton, 1974.

Cogliano, Francis D. *Thomas Jefferson: Reputation and Legacy.* Charlottesville: University of Virginia Press, 2006.

Frontline. "1868: The Memoirs of Israel Jefferson." From "Life among the Lowly, No. 3," *Pike County* (Ohio) *Republican*, December 25, 1873.

——. "1873: The Memoirs of Madison Hemings." From "Life among the Lowly, No. 1," *Pike County* (Ohio) *Republican*, March 13, 1873. pbs.org/wgbh/pages/frontline/shows/jefferson/cron/1873march.html.

——. "Interview: Lucia Cinder Stanton." pbs.org/wgbh/pages/frontline/shows/jefferson/interviews/stanton.html.

Gordon-Reed, Annette. *The Hemingses of Monticello: An American Family.* New York: Norton, 2008.

——. *Thomas Jefferson and Sally Hemings: An American Controversy.* Charlottesville: University Press of Virginia, 1997.

Jefferson, Isaac. *Memoirs of a Monticello Slave.* Edited by Rayford W. Logan. Charlottesville: University of Virginia Press, 1951.

Kukla, Jon. *Mr. Jefferson's Women.* New York: Knopf, 2007.

Monticello. "Sally Hemings." monticello.org/plantation/lives/sallyhemings.html.

Scharff, Virginia. *The Women Jefferson Loved.* New York: HarperCollins, 2010.

Stanton, Lucia. *Free Some Day: The African-American Families of Monticello.* Charlottesville, VA: Thomas Jefferson Foundation, 2000.

AGRIPPA HULL

Egleston, Thomas. *The Life of John Paterson.* 2nd ed. New York: G. P. Putnam's Sons: 1898, pp. 308–10. archive.org/stream/lifejohnpaters003eglegoog#page/n366/mode/2up/search/Grippy.

Jones, Electa. *Stockbridge, Past and Present.* Springfield, MA: Samuel Bowles, 1854, pp. 240–42.

Kaplan, Sidney, and Emma Nogrady Kaplan. *The Black Presence in the Era of the American Revolution*, pp. 40–44.

Nash, Gary B. "Agrippa Hull, Revolutionary Patriot." BlackPast.org. blackpast.org/?q=perspectives/agrippa-hull-revolutionary-patriot.

Nash, Gary B., and Graham Russell Gao Hodges. *Friends of Liberty: Thomas Jefferson, Tadeusz Kościuszko, and Agrippa Hull; A Tale of Three Patriots, Two Revolutions, and a Tragic Betrayal of Freedom in the New Nation.* New York: Basic Books, 2008.

ONA JUDGE

Adams, T. H. "Washington's Runaway Slave." *The Granite Freeman*, Concord, New Hampshire (May 22, 1845); reprinted in *Frank W. Miller's Portsmouth New Hampshire Weekly*, June 2, 1877, under the title "Washington's Runaway Slave, and How Portsmouth Freed Her." USHistory.org. ushistory.org/presidentshouse/slaves/oneyinterview.htm.

Chase, Benjamin. "1846 Interview with Ona Judge Staines." A letter to the editor in *The Liberator*, January 1, 1847, as quoted in *Slave Testimony: Two Centuries of Letters, Speeches, Interviews, and Autobiographies*, edited by John W. Blassingame. Baton Rouge: Louisiana State University Press, 1977, pp. 248–50. ushistory.org/presidentshouse/slaves/oneyinterview.htm.

Gerson, Evelyn. "Ona Judge Staines: A Thirst for Complete Freedom and Her Escape from President Washington." SeacoastNH.com. seacoastnh.com/blackhistory/ona.html.

Hirschfeld, Fritz. *George Washington and Slavery: A Documentary Portrayal*. Columbia: University of Missouri Press, 1997, pp. 112–17.

Wiencek, Henry. *An Imperfect God: George Washington, His Slaves, and the Creation of America*. New York: Farrar, Straus and Giroux, 2003.

BOSTON KING

Caretta, Vincent, ed. *Unchained Voices: An Anthology of Black Authors in the English-Speaking World of the 18th Century*. Lexington: University Press of Kentucky, 1996.

Dictionary of Canadian Biography. Vol. 5 (1801–1820). biographi.ca/en/bio/king_boston_5E.html.

King, Boston. *Memoirs of the Life of Boston King, a Black Preacher*. Antislavery Literature. antislavery.eserver.org/narratives/boston_king/memoirs-of-boston-king-a-black-preacher.html/?searchterm=Boston%20King.

Wilson, Ellen Gibson. *The Loyal Blacks*.

JOHN KIZELL

Lowther, Kevin G. *The African American Odyssey of John Kizell: A South Carolina Slave Returns to Fight the Slave Trade in His African Homeland*. Columbia: University of South Carolina Press, 2011.

Sixth Report of the Directors of the African Institution, March 1812, London. "Extracts from the Correspondence of Mr. John Kizell with Governor Columbine, Respecting His Negotiations with the Chiefs in the River Sherbro, and Giving an Account of That River," pp. 113–54.

Special Report of the Directors of the African Institution, April 12, 1815, London, pp. 32–37.

JAMES ARMISTEAD LAFAYETTE

Abdul-Jabbar, Kareem, and Alan Steinberg. *Black Profiles in Courage: A Legacy of African-American Achievement*. New York: William Morrow, 1996, pp. 32–34.

Kaplan, Sidney, and Emma Nogrady Kaplan. *The Black Presence in the Era of the American Revolution*, pp. 37–40.

Logan, Rayford W., and Michael R. Winston, eds. *Dictionary of American Negro Biography*. New York: Norton, 1982, pp. 16–17.

Waller, James. "Espionage: Slave Turned Double Agent: James Armistead Lafayette." *Military History*, August 1994.

Ward, Harry M. *For Virginia and for Independence: Twenty-Eight Revolutionary War Soldiers from the Old Dominion*. Jefferson, NC: McFarland, 2011.

Wiencek, Henry. *An Imperfect God: George Washington, His Slaves, and the Creation of America*. New York: Farrar, Straus and Giroux, 2003.

JARENA LEE

Africans in America. "Catherine Brekus on Jarena Lee." Interview with Professor Catherine Brekus, associate professor, University of Chicago Divinity School. pbs.org/wgbh/aia/part3/3i3127.html.

Andrews, William L., ed. *Sisters of the Spirit: Three Black Women's Autobiographies of the Nineteenth Century*. Bloomington: Indiana University Press, 1986.

Davidson, Phebe. "Jarena Lee." *Legacy: A Journal of American Women Writers* 10, no. 2 (1993).

Lee, Jarena. *Religious Experience and Journal of Mrs. Jarena Lee, Giving an Account of Her Call to Preach the Gospel*. Philadelphia: privately printed, 1840.

MARY PERTH

The Evangelical Magazine. "Singular Piety in a Female African: Letter from the Rev. Mr. Clark, Chaplain to the Sierra-Leone Establishment. To His Father." Vol. 4, 1796, pp. 460–64.

Pybus, Cassandra. *Epic Journeys of Freedom: Runaway Slaves of the American Revolution and Their Global Quest for Liberty*.

———. "Mary Perth, Harry Washington, and Moses Wilkinson: Black Methodists Who Escaped from Slavery and Founded a Nation." In *Revolutionary Founders: Rebels, Radicals, and Reformers in the Making of a Nation*, edited by Alfred F. Young, Gary B. Nash, and Ray Raphael, pp. 155–68.

———. "'One Militant Saint': The Much Traveled Life of Mary Perth." *Journal of Colonialism and Colonial History* 9, no. 3 (Winter 2008).

PHILLIS WHEATLEY

African Americans and the End of Slavery in Massachusetts. "Phillis Wheatley." Massachusetts Historical Society. masshist.org/endofslavery/index.php?id=57.

Carretta, Vincent. *Phillis Wheatley: Biography of a Genius in Bondage.* Athens: University of Georgia Press, 2011.

Gates, Henry Louis, Jr. *The Trials of Phillis Wheatley: America's First Black Poet and Her Encounters with the Founding Fathers.* New York: Basic Civitas Books, 2003.

Hirschfeld, Fritz. *George Washington and Slavery: A Documentary Portrayal.* Columbia: University of Missouri Press, 1997, pp. 86–95.

Kaplan, Sidney, and Emma Nogrady Kaplan. *The Black Presence in the Era of the American Revolution,* pp. 170–91.

Robinson, William H. *Phillis Wheatley in the Black American Beginnings.* Detroit: Broadside Press, 1975.

Waldstreicher, David. "Phillis Wheatley: The Poet Who Challenged the American Revolutionaries." In *Revolutionary Founders: Rebels, Radicals, and Reformers in the Making of the Nation,* edited by Alfred F. Young, Gary B. Nash, and Ray Raphael, pp. 97–113.

Wheatley, Phillis. *The Poems of Phillis Wheatley.* Edited by Julian D. Mason Jr. Chapel Hill: University of North Carolina Press, 1989.

Wheatley, Phillis. *Poems on Various Subjects, Religious and Moral.* London: A. Bell, 1773. memory.loc.gov/cgi-bin/ampage?collId=ody_rbcmisc&fileName=ody/ody0215/ody-0215page.db&recNum=2&itemLink=%2Fammem%2Faaohtml%2Fexhibit%2Faopart2.html%400215&linkText=9.

Young, Margaret Blair. "Phillis Wheatley (1754–1784)." BlackPast.org. blackpast.org/?q=aah/wheatley-phillis-1754-1784.

FOR YOUNG READERS

Allen, Thomas B. *George Washington, Spymaster: How the Americans Outspied the British and Won the Revolutionary War.* Washington, DC: National Geographic, 2004.

Blair, Margaret Whitman. *Liberty or Death: The Surprising Story of Runaway Slaves Who Sided with the British during the American Revolution.* Washington, DC: National Geographic, 2010.

Davis, Burke. *Black Heroes of the American Revolution.* New York: Odyssey Books, 1976.

Delano, Marfé Ferguson. *Master George's People: George Washington, His Slaves, and His Revolutionary Transformation.* Washington, DC: National Geographic, 2013.

Diamond, Arthur. *Paul Cuffe: Merchant and Abolitionist*. Black Americans of Achievement. New York: Chelsea House, 1989.

———. *Prince Hall: Social Reformer*. Black Americans of Achievement. New York: Chelsea House, 1992.

Doak, Robin S. *Phillis Wheatley: Slave and Poet*. Minneapolis: Compass Point Books, 2006.

Egger-Bovet, Howard, and Marlene Smith-Baranzini. *Book of the American Revolution*. Brown Paper School USKids History. Boston: Little, Brown, 1994.

Fleming, Thomas. *Everybody's Revolution: A New Look at the People Who Won America's Freedom*. New York: Scholastic, 2006.

Holton, Woody. *Black Americans in the Revolutionary Era: A Brief History with Documents*. Boston: Bedford/St. Martin's, 2009.

Klots, Steve. *Richard Allen: Religious Leader and Social Activist*. New York: Chelsea House, 1991.

Lanier, Shannon, and Jane Feldman, comps. *Jefferson's Children: The Story of One American Family*. New York: Random House, 2000.

Littlefield, Daniel C. *Revolutionary Citizens: African Americans, 1776–1804*. New York: Oxford University Press, 1997.

Maestro, Betsy. *Liberty or Death: The American Revolution, 1763–1783*. New York: HarperCollins, 2005.

Sheinkin, Steve. *King George: What Was His Problem?* New York: Roaring Brook Press, 2008.

Woelfle, Gretchen. *Mumbet's Declaration of Independence*. Minneapolis: Carolrhoda Books, 2014.

WEBSITES[*]

Africans in America. The Revolutionary War. pbs.org/wgbh/aia/part2/2narr4.html.

Antislavery Literature. antislavery.eserver.org.

Black Loyalist Heritage Society. Information on the Black Loyalist Heritage Centre and Historical Site in Birchtown, Nova Scotia, Canada; digital photo collections; and more. blackloyalist.com.

Freedom on the Move: a database of runaway slaves. Freedomonthemove.org

Geography of Slavery in Virginia, The. www2.vcdh.virginia.edu/gos/

Massachusetts Historical Society. African Americans and the End of Slavery in Massachusetts. masshist.org/endofslavery/index.php.

Slavery in the North. The history of slavery in the northern colonies in the 1600s through the mid-1800s. slavenorth.com/index.html.

United Empire Loyalists. en.citizendium.org/wiki/United_Empire_Loyalists.

*Websites active at time of publication

SOURCE NOTES*

The source of each quotation in this book is found below. The citation indicates the first words of the quotation and its document source. The document sources are listed either in the bibliography or below.

INTRODUCTION (page 6)

"Liberty, when it begins . . .": letter from George Washington to James Madison, March 2, 1788, New York Public Library Digital Collections, digitalcollections.nypl.org/items/8bc30ebb-0764-a3e0-e040-e00a180639a9#/?uuid=8bc30ebb-0765-a3e0-e040-e00a180639a9.

PART ONE: FIGHTING A WAR FOR FREEDOM (page 8)

"All Negroes that fly . . .": Pybus, *Epic Journeys*, p. 28.

BOSTON KING (page 14)

"My father was stolen . . .": King, p. 105, antislavery.eserver.org/narratives/boston_king/bostonkingproof.pdf/.
"The horrible sin of Swearing and Cursing" and "bad company.": same as above, p. 106.
"I dreamt that the world . . ." and "into the greatest . . .": same as above.
"beat me severely . . .": same as above.
"I began to acquire . . .": same as above, p. 107.
"I determined to . . . throw myself . . .": same as above.
"rejoicing that it was in my power . . .": same as above.
"but the wages were so low . . .": same as above, p. 109.
"But alas, all these enjoyments . . .": same as above, p. 110.
"This was a terrifying sight . . .": same as above.
"I am sure I saw . . .": same as above.
"There is no . . .": same as above.
"My friends rejoiced . . .": same as above, p. 157.
"This dreadful rumour . . .": same as above.
"Peace be unto . . ." and "All my doubts . . .": same as above, p. 160.
"was conscious of . . .": same as above, p. 161.
"being pinched with hunger . . .": same as above, p. 210.
"distressing, owing to their . . .": same as above.
"great satisfaction.": same as above, p. 213.

*Websites active at time of publication

"a gentleman, who gave . . .": same as above.

"The majority of the men . . .": Wilson, p. 201.

"It was not for the . . .": King, p. 213.

"wise and judicious people . . ." and "ignorance and inability": same as above, p. 264.

"I found a more . . .": same as above.

"[I] endeavoured to acquire . . .": same as above.

"I did not believe . . .": same as above.

AGRIPPA HULL (page 28)

"Stature, 5 ft., 7 in. . . .": Nash, *Friends of Liberty*, pp. 19, 21.

"intelligent and unusually bright" and "His aptness and wit . . .": Egleston, p. 308.

"stretched out on the sofa . . .": Nash, *Friends of Liberty*, pp. 263–64.

"Whip me, kill me . . ." and "Rise, Prince . . .": Egleston, p. 309.

"The whole country is . . .": Nash, *Friends of Liberty*, p. 65.

"but poverty in their pockets.": same as above, p. 82.

"Hull's presence at weddings . . ." and "He wedged . . .": Jones, p. 241.

"always trimming . . .": Nash, *Friends of Liberty*, p. 196.

"Well, how do you like . . ." to "Sir . . .": Jones, p. 242.

"had no cringing servility . . .": same as above, p. 241.

"It is not the cover . . .": same as above, p. 242.

"He felt deeply . . .": same as above.

"slightly bent by . . ." and "the most noticed . . .": Nash, *Friends of Liberty*, pp. 262, 263.

"If you wish it . . .": same as above, p. 263.

"He was a lovely man.": same as above, p. 264.

"From that day to this . . .": same as above, p. 266.

JAMES ARMISTEAD LAFAYETTE (page 38)

"[Lafayette] called to him . . .": Waller, p. 18.

"His intelligences from . . .": Ward, p. 157.

"A correspondent of mine . . ." and "His Lordship . . .": Wiencek, p. 252.

"We have been beating . . .": *Victory at Yorktown: The Campaign That Won the Revolution*, by Richard M. Ketchum, New York: Henry Holt, 2004, p. 249.

"Being impelled by . . ." to "praying that an act . . .": Ward, p. 157.

"I would never have drawn . . .": Hirschfeld, p. 121.

"This is to Certify. . .": Ward, p. 157.

"the just right . . ." to "humbly intreats . . .": same as above, pp. 157–58.

"broken, and much worn": same as above, p. 158.

PHILLIS WHEATLEY (page 52)

"assure the World, that the Poems . . .": Wheatley, African American Odyssey,
　　　Library of Congress, memory.loc.gov/cgi-bin/ampage?collId=ody_rbcmisc
　　　&fileName=ody/ody0215/ody0215page.db&recNum=8&itemLink=r%3F-
　　　ammem%2FAMALL%3A%40field%28NUMBER%2B%40oband%28rbcmis-
　　　c%2Body0215%29%29&linkText=0.

"I was a poor . . .": letter from Wheatley to Obour Tanner, March 21, 1774,
　　　Massachusetts Historical Society, masshist.org/database/viewer.php?item_
　　　id=775&img_step=1&mode=dual#page1.

"Her own curiosity . . .": African American Odyssey, Library of Congress,
　　　memory.loc.gov/cgi-bin/ampage?collId=ody_rbcmisc&fileName=ody/ody
　　　0215/ody0215page.db&recNum=7&itemLink=r%3Fammem%2FAMALL
　　　%3A%40field%28NUMBER%2B%40oband%28rbcmisc%2Body0215%29%
　　　29&linkText=0.

"without rising or . . .": Kaplan, p. 177.

"Did Fear and Danger . . .": Wheatley, p. 115.

"'Twas mercy brought . . .": Wheatley, African American Odyssey, Library of Congress,
　　　p. 18, memory.loc.gov/cgi-bin/ampage?collId=ody_rbcmisc&fileName=ody/
　　　ody0215/ody0215page.db&recNum=19&itemLink=r?ammem/AMALL:@
　　　field(NUMBER+@band(rbcmisc+ody0215))&linkText-0.

"Long as in . . .": Gates, pp. 20–21.

"Hail, happy day . . .": Wheatley, African American Odyssey, Library of Congress,
　　　pp. 73–74, memory.loc.gov/cgi-bin/ampage?collId=ody_rbcmisc&fileName-
　　　=ody/ody0215/ody0215page.db&recNum=74&itemLink=r?ammem/AMALL:@
　　　field(NUMBER+@band(rbcmisc+ody0215))&linkText=0.

"I, young in life . . .": Wheatley, same as above, p. 74, memory.loc.gov/cgi-bin/
　　　ampage?collId=ody_rbcmisc&fileName=ody/ody0215/ody0215page.db&rec
　　　Num=75&itemLink=r?ammem/AMALL:@field(NUMBER+@band(rbcmisc+od
　　　y0215))&linkText=0.

"I hope the correspondence . . .": Wheatley, p. 190.

"very dark, pious . . .": Wheatley, p. 190.

"Till we meet . . .": same as above.

"I recd. . . .": letter from Wheatley to Tanner, May 6, 1774,
　　　Massachusetts Historical Society, masshist.org/database/viewer. php?item_
　　　id=776&img_step=1&mode=transcript#page1.

"WE whose Names . . .": Wheatley, African American Odyssey,Library of Congress,
　　　memory.loc.gov/cgi-binampage?collId=ody_rbcmisc&fileName=ody/ody0215/
　　　ody0215page.db&recNum=8&itemLink=r%3Famem%2FAMALL3A%40field

%28NUMBER%2B%40band%28rbcmisc%2Body0215%29%29&linkText=0.

"When first thy pencil . . .": Wheatley, same as above, p. 114, memory.loc.gov/cgi-bin/
        ampage?collId=ody_rbcmisc&fileName=ody/ody0215/
        ody0215page.db&recNum=115&itemLink=r?ammem/
        AMALL:@field(NUMBER+@band(rbcmisc+))&linkText=0.

"The Friends I found . . .": Wheatley, p. 198.

"too many things . . .": letter from Wheatley to David Worcester, October 18, 1773,
        Massachusetts Historical Society, masshist.org/database/
        viewer.php?item_id=771&img_step=1&mode=dual#page1.

"I have lately met. . .": letter from Wheatley to Tanner, March 21, 1774,
        Massachusetts Historical Society, masshist.org/database/viewer.
        php?item_id=775&img_step=1&mode=dual#page1.

"I beg the favour . . .": letter from Wheatley to Worcester, October 18, 1773,
        same as above, masshist.org/database/viewer.
        php?item_id=771&img_step=1&mode=transcript#page1.

"In every human Breast . . .": Wheatley, p. 204.

"the strange Absurdity . . .": same as above.

"Possibly the Ambition . . ." to "craftiness of the enemies . . .": letter from Wheatley to
        Tanner, 1776, Wikipedia, en.wikipedia.org/wiki/File:Phillis_wheatley_let-
        ter_to_obour_tanner_1776_front.jpg.

"I thank you . . ." to "to give the World . . .": Wheatley, p. 165.

"Thee, first in place . . .": same as above, p. 167.

"Poor Phillis . . .": Robinson, p. 20.

"Tho' I have been silent . . .": letter from Wheatley to Tanner, May 10, 1779,
        Massachusetts Historical Society, masshist.org/database/viewer.
        php?item_id=778&img_step=1&mode=dual#page1.

"savage Troops": Wheatley, p. 176.

"To every Realm . . .": same as above, p. 177.

"So sweetly blooming . . .": same as above, p. 179.

ELIZABETH "MUMBET" FREEMAN (page 70)

"a shrew untameable" and "the most despotic . . .": Sedgwick, p. 418, play.google.com/
        books/reader?id=8-&printsec=frontcover&output=reader&hl=en&pg=GBS.
        PA418.

"Thief!" and "I had a bad arm . . .": same as above.

"Any time, any time . . .": same as above, p. 421.

"RESOLVED, That mankind . . .": Constitution Society, constitution.org/bcp/sheffield_
        declaration.html.

"Resolved, That the great end . . .": same as above.

"Article I. All men . . .": Who We Are, National Humanities Institute, nhinet.org/ccs/docs/ma-1780.htm.

"Sir, I heard . . .": Sedgwick, p. 421, play.google.com/books/reader?id-=8-ARAAAAYAA&printsec=frontcover&output=reader&hl=en&pg=GBS.PA418.

"seeking and obtaining . . .": Who We Are, National Humanities Institute, nhinet.org/ccs/docs/ma-1780.htm.

"ELIZABETH FREEMAN (known by . . .": same as above, p. 424.

PRINCE HALL (page 80)

"Prince Hall has lived . . .": Conference of Grand Masters, conferenceofgrandmasterspha.org/gmasters_history.asp.

"Boston April the 24 1777 . . .": Africans in America, pbs.org/wgbh/aia/part2/2h44t.html.

"the Honorable Counsel . . .": Massachusetts Historical Society, masshist.org/database/viewer.php?item_id=557&mode=nav.

"The petition of A Great Number . . .": same as above.

"Our Constitution of Govmt . . .": same as above, masshist.org/database/viewer.php?item_id=630&img_step=1&br=1&mode=transcript#page1.

"The African Lodge . . .": Massachusetts Historical Society, Belknap Papers, pp. 210–11, masshist.org/database/viewer.php?item_id=693&mode=transcript&img_step=20#page20.

"Our title . . .": Kaplan, pp. 204–5.

"A tall, lean Negro . . .": Haywood, p. 170.

"knowing by Experience . . .": Massachusetts Historical Society, masshist.org/database/viewer.php?item_id=670&img_step=1&mode=dual#page1.

"the right to enjoy . . .": Kaplan, p. 209.

"October 4, 1796 . . .": Wesley, p. 200.

"a very intelligent black man": Massachusetts Historical Society, masshist.org/database/viewer.php?item_id=693&mode=transcript&img_step=9#page9.

"Does harmony . . ." to "As to our associating . . .": Massachusetts Historical Society, Belknap Papers, pp. 209–10, masshist.org/database/viewer.php?item_id=693&mode=transcript&img_step=20#page19.

"Let us pray God . . .": BlackPast.org, blackpast.org/?q=1797-prince-hall-speaks-african-lodge-cambridge-massachusetts.

MARY PERTH (page 96)

"If we permit . . .": Pybus, "'One Militant Saint,'" p. 1.

"All Negroes that fly . . .": Pybus, *Epic Journeys*, p. 28.

"[carry] away any negroes . . .": A Century of Lawmaking: U.S. Congressional Documents and Debates, 1774–1875, p. 83, American Memory, Library of Congress, memory.loc.gov/cgi-bin/ampage?collId=llsl&fileName=008/llsl008. db&recNum=96.

"reduce themselves . . .": Pybus, *Epic Journeys*, p. 67.

"The Negroes in question . . .": same as above, p. 68.

"stout wench": Wilson, p. 75.

"pious frenzy": same as above, p. 120.

"Awake! and sing the song . . .": same as above, p. 233.

"We have feeling . . .": same as above, p. 283.

"There is one old woman . . .": *The Evangelical Magazine*, pp. 461–63.

"the good old woman": Pybus, "'One Militant Saint,'" p. 6.

"We don't want you . . .": same as above.

"She is the best . . .": *The Evangelical Magazine*, pp. 461–63.

"vain, worldly, and arrogant . . ." and "most unchristian . . .": Pybus, "'One Militant Saint,'" pp. 6–7.

"the common Methodist cant.": same as above, p. 7.

"unhinge her mind . . ." and "little attentive . . .": same as above.

"She seemed not . . .": Wilson, p. 377.

ONA JUDGE (page 108)

"She has been . . .": Hirschfeld, p. 113.

"I had friends . . .": Adams.

"Whilst they were packing . . .": same as above.

"ABSCONDED . . ." to "to any person": *Pennsylvania Gazette and Daily Advertiser*, May 24, 1796.

"Mrs. Washington's girl": *Philadelphia Household Account Book*, 5/10/1796.

"I never told . . .": Adams.

"a free mulattoe . . ." and "Whether this last . . .": letter from Thomas Lee Jr. to George Washington, June 28, 1796, Mount Vernon Association.

"To seize, and put her . . .": Hirschfeld, p. 113.

"a thirst for . . ." and "She should rather suffer . . .": same as above, p. 114.

"I am free now . . ." and "They never troubled . . .": Adams.

"I am free, and have, I trust . . .": same as above.

SALLY HEMINGS (page 120)

"Betty was a bright . . .": Isaac Jefferson, Internet Archive, p. 10, archive.org/stream/
        memoirsofamontic031158mbp/memoirsofamontic031158mbp_djvu.txt.

"good naturd" and "quite a child": letter from Abigail Adams to Thomas Jefferson,
        June 27, 1787, Founders Online, founders.archives.gov/documents/
        Jefferson/01-11-02-0420.

"Sally was very handsome . . ." and "mighty near white": Isaac Jefferson Internet
        Archive, p. 10, archive.org/stream/memoirsofamontic031158mbp/
        memoirsofamontic031158mbp_djvu.txt.

"Dashing Sally": Gordon-Reed, Thomas Jefferson, p. 160.

"Sally Hemings . . . was employed . . .": Israel Jefferson, Frontline, pbs.org/wgbh/pages/
        frontline/shows/jefferson/cron/1873israel.html.

"promised [Sally] extraordinary privileges . . .": Madison Hemings, Frontline, pbs.org/
        wgbh/pages/frontline/shows/jefferson/cron/1873march.html.

"lived but a . . .": same as above.

"When Madison Hemings . . .": Israel Jefferson, pbs.org/wgbh/pages/frontline/shows/
        jefferson/cron/1873israel.html.

"Dusky Sally": Gordon-Reed, *The Hemingses*, p. 583.

"gentleman dining with Mr. Jefferson . . .": letter from Henry S. Randall to James
        Parton, June 1, 1868, Frontline, pbs.org/wgbh/pages/frontline/shows/jeffer-
        son/cron/1868randall.html.

"It was her duty . . .": Madison Hemings, pbs.org/wgbh/pages/frontline/shows/
        jefferson/cron/1873march.html.

"was uniformly kind . . ." and "fatherly affection . . .": same as above.

"we were free . . .": same as above.

"Jefferson . . . freed one girl . . .": Bacon, Frontline, pbs.org/wgbh/pages/frontline/
        shows/jefferson/slaves/bacon.html.

"Beverly run away . . .": *Farm Book* by Thomas Jefferson, 1774–1824, p. 130,
        Massachusetts Historical Society, masshist.org/thomasjeffer-
        sonpapers/doc?id=farm_130&archive=farm&query=Beverly%20
        run&tag=text&num=10&rec=2&numRecs=30#firstmatch.

"His death . . .": Israel Jefferson, pbs.org/wgbh/pages/frontline/shows/jefferson/
        cron/1873israel.html.

PAUL CUFFE (page 138)

"Robbed of every thing . . .": *Belfast Monthly Magazine*, p. 285.

"An old friend . . .": same as above.

"The petition of . . .": Holton, pp. 75–76.

"and by law not subject . . .": Thomas, p. 10.

"Paul Cuff [is] the owner . . .": same as above, pp. 26–27.

"the people were filled . . ." and "excite a . . .": *Belfast Monthly Magazine*, p. 288.

"their conduct has always . . .": same as above, p. 291.

"Paul set himself to work . . .": same as above.

"A person like Paul Cuffe . . .": Thomas, p. 44.

"I feel Very febel . . ." and "But blessed . . .": Wiggins, p. 78.

"The Dust of Africa . . .": same as above, p. 104.

"Caught 1 Dolfin . . .": same as above, p. 105.

"Which Was a Pleasing . . .": Thomas, p. 52.

"The industery on their farmes . . ." and "become mannegers . . .": Wiggins, p. 119.

"On the first of . . .": *Edinburgh Review*, August 1811, Kaplan, p. 158.

"The Brig *Traveller* . . .": Thomas, p. 57.

"His person is tall . . .": *Belfast Monthly Magazine*, p. 292.

"dressed in . . .": Diamond, *Paul Cuffe*, p. 72.

"He seems like a man . . .": Lowther, p. 189.

"When men are like Lions . . .": Wiggins, p. 192.

"If the Wind . . .": Thomas, p. 72.

"James, I have been put . . .": same as above, p. 74.

"Was travelling . . .": Wiggins, p. 213.

"not as I thought myself . . .": same as above, p. 75.

"There Was a Part . . .": same as above, p. 216.

"they were in high Spirits . . ." to "Go and fill . . .": same as above, p. 434.

"Just arrived Captured . . .": same as above, p. 412.

"A sound understanding . . .": *Belfast Monthly Magazine*, p. 292.

JOHN KIZELL (page 154)

"I have seen a man . . .": *Sixth Report of the Directors of the African Institution*, p. 125.

"[Charleston slaves] did not act . . .": Lowther, p. 19.

"[Never would the British . . .": Pybus, *Epic Journeys*, p. 67.

"The generality . . .": Lowther, p. 115.

"We cannot do . . .": same as above, pp. 142–43.

"men of at best . . .": same as above, p. 140.

"more thinking": Lowther, p. 136.

"In the generosity . . .": same as above, p. 137.

"This tree . . .": *Sixth Report*, pp. 136, 137.

"whenever he looked . . .": Lowther, p. 143.

"one of yourselves . . .": *Sixth Report*, p. 114.

"I told them that . . .": same as above, p. 120.

"the Governor did not . . ." and "clapped their hands . . .": same as above, p. 141.

"At one time . . .": same as above, p. 118.

"They inquired, 'If you come . . .": same as above, p. 116.

"to rid our country . . .": Thomas, p. 111.

"Africa is the land . . .": Lowther, p. 209.

"the greater part of . . .": same as above.

"wide and long . . .": same as above, p. 218.

"God has sent me here . . .": same as above.

"No man's heart . . .": same as above, pp. 209–10.

"nothing but imposters . . .": same as above, p. 222.

"He is an intelligent man . . .": *Sixth Report*, p. 145.

RICHARD ALLEN (page 168)

"Negro Richard": Nash, "New Light on Richard Allen," p. 338.

"All of a sudden . . .": Allen, p. 5.

"what the world called . . .": same as above, p. 6.

"he was convinced . . ." and "their honesty . . .": same as above.

"Thou art weighed . . .": same as above, p. 7.

"Slavery is a bitter pill . . .": same as above.

"When I left . . .": same as above.

"many happy seasons . . .": same as above, p. 8.

"I Do hereby . . .": Nash, "New Light on Richard Allen," p. 338.

"I . . . preached on Sabbath . . .": Allen, p. 9.

"I soon saw . . .": same as above, p. 12.

"an orderly and . . .": Newman, *Freedom's Prophet*, p. 60.

"We have suffered equally . . .": Allen, pp. 37–38.

"Surely our task . . .": same as above, p. 40.

"Having, during the prevalence . . .": same as above, p. 44.

"We have many unprovoked . . .": same as above, p. 36.

"If you love your children . . .": same as above, p. 46.

"the favour and love . . .": same as above, p. 47.

"Much depends upon us . . .": same as above, p. 48.

"I feel an inexpressible . . .": same as above, pp. 48–49.

"We, my friends . . .": "Eulogy of George Washington" by Richard Allen, USHistory.org, ushistory.org/presidentshouse/history/alleneulogy.htm.

"We all went out . . .": Allen, p. 13.

"were the first people . . .": same as above, p. 17.

"plain and simple . . ." and "suits best . . .": same as above, p. 16.

"I could not be . . .": same as above.

"[They] might deny us . . .": same as above, p. 18.

"Mark [see] the perfect man . . .": same as above, p. 3.

"WHEREAS our ancestors . . .": Klots, p. 77.

"His house was never shut . . .": *History of the African Methodist Episcopal Church*, by Daniel A. Payne, Nashville: A. M. E. Sunday School Union, 1891, p. 84, docsouth.unc.edu/church/payne/payne.html.

"This land which we have . . .": Newman, *Freedom's Prophet*, p. 150.

JARENA LEE (page 184)

"Go preach . . ." to "there stood before me . . .": Lee, pp. 10–11.

"And it shall come . . .": same as above, p. 3.

"Lord, I am vile . . .": same as above.

"I was driven . . ." and "drowning would be . . ." and "the unseen arm" and "was exceedingly . . .": same as above, p. 4.

"this is the people . . .": same as above, p. 5.

"Though hundreds were present . . .": same as above.

"The Lord had revealed . . .": same as above, p. 11.

"that holy energy . . .": same as above.

"never found that agreement . . .": same as above, p. 13.

"One thing . . .": same as above, p. 14.

"Some wept . . .": same as above, p. 18.

"By the instrumentality . . .": same as above.

"not a thought . . .": same as above.

"he did not believe . . ." and "he became greatly . . .": same as above, p. 19.

"If an ass reproved . . .": same as above, p. 23.

"Glory to God's dear . . .": same as above, p. 22.

"The oppositions I met . . ." and "I embraced . . .": same as above, p. 24.

"My mind soon . . .": same as above, p. 40.

"The thought . . .": same as above, p. 33.

"This was the first time . . .": same as above, p. 49.

"without the advantages . . .": same as above, p. 69.

"The wickedness of . . .": same as above, p. 63.

"I had but three . . .": same as above, p. 64.

"fell to the floor . . ." and "it was a dull . . .": same as above, p. 87.

"We might call them . . .": same as above, p. 51.

"my heart glows with joy . . .": same as above, p. 39.

"very rich as regards . . ." and "a broken heart . . .": same as above, p. 56.

"for the cause . . ." and "much opposition . . .": same as above, p. 61.

"Glory to God for . . .": same as above, p. 56.

"corrected it for . . .": same as above, p. 66.

"It is impossible . . .": Andrews, p. 6.

"carnal amusements": Lee, p. 69.

"I commenced travelling . . .": same as above, p. 97.

"Why should it be thought . . .": same as above, p. 11.

"As for me . . .": same as above, p. 12.

EPILOGUE: ECHOES OF THE CRY FOR FREEDOM
(page 198)

"I, young in life . . .": Wheatley, African American Odyssey, Library of Congress, p. 74, memory.loc.gov/cgi-bin/ampage?collId=ody_rbcmisc&fileName=ody/ody0215/ody0215page.db&recNum=75&itemLink=r?ammem/AMALL:@field(NUMBER+@band(rbcmisc+ody0215))&linkText=0.

"Their aspirings and little . . .": Nash, *Race and Revolution*, p. 73.

"They dared to organize . . .": same as above.

INDEX

Gretchen Woelfle is the author of award-winning fiction and nonfiction books for young readers, including *Jeannette Rankin: Political Pioneer*; *Write On, Mercy!: The Secret Life of Mercy Otis Warren*; and *Mumbet's Declaration of Independence*. When she is not traveling the world hunting for stories, Gretchen lives in Los Angeles, California, writing more biographies of unconventional people. Visit gretchenwoelfle.com.

R. Gregory Christie has illustrated more than fifty books for young adults and children. His work has won a *New York Times* 10 Best Illustrated Children's Books of the Year Award, the Coretta Scott King Honor Award in Illustration, an NAACP Image Award, the Boston Globe–Horn Book Award, and the Theodor Seuss Geisel Award. He currently works as a freelance illustrator and operates his store of autographed children's books, GAS-Art Gifts, located in Decatur, Georgia. He lives near Atlanta. Visit gas-art.com.